Luciano Giannini

Communication and Relationships:

Luciano Giannini

Communication and Relationships:

The realisation of actions initiated on digital social networks (the case of Pref's)

ScienciaScripts

Imprint
Any brand names and product names mentioned in this book are subject to trademark, brand or patent protection and are trademarks or registered trademarks of their respective holders. The use of brand names, product names, common names, trade names, product descriptions etc. even without a particular marking in this work is in no way to be construed to mean that such names may be regarded as unrestricted in respect of trademark and brand protection legislation and could thus be used by anyone.

Cover image: www.ingimage.com

This book is a translation from the original published under ISBN 978-3-330-99578-9.

Publisher:
Sciencia Scripts
is a trademark of
Dodo Books Indian Ocean Ltd. and OmniScriptum S.R.L publishing group

120 High Road, East Finchley, London, N2 9ED, United Kingdom
Str. Armeneasca 28/1, office 1, Chisinau MD-2012, Republic of Moldova, Europe
Managing Directors: Ieva Konstantinova, Victoria Ursu
info@omniscriptum.com

Printed at: see last page
ISBN: 978-620-8-58691-1

I dedicate this work to my father, Paolo Giannini, and my father-in-law, Lídio Dudek, who, for different reasons, will not be able to follow this very important process in my life, but I'm sure they will be proud to see this achievement.

ACKNOWLEDGEMENTS

Many thanks to everyone who played a part in this achievement.

- To the professors and colleagues of the Communication and Languages Programme at the Tuiuti University of Paraná,
- To Prof Dr Geraldo Pieroni for his lectures and contributions to this work, from the very first drafts. Also for agreeing to sit on the exam board and for his valuable guidance during the qualification process.
- To Professor Dr Claudia Quadros for accepting the invitation to sit on the panel and for her guidance and contributions during the qualification process.
- To Professor Dr Carlos Eduardo Marquioni, who was much more than an advisor. He was there at important moments, advising me and guiding this "disorientated" man to find the best path.
- To the Pref's, represented by professionals Álvaro Borba, Camila Braga and especially Jana Santos, who were helpful and fundamental in providing the materials and information that made up this research.
- To my family, be it my blood family or my extended family (lol), who have always supported and encouraged me in my development plans.
- Especially to my wonderful wife, Cristiane Dudek Giannini, who was there every step of the way, supporting me, encouraging me, not letting me give up and always getting the best out of me. Thank you! I love you!

"Beating someone makes you a winner;

Beating yourself makes you invincible.

(MORIHEI UESHIBA, founder of Aikido)

SUMMARY

The research analytically investigates, in the context of a digital social network (RECUERO, 2009), to what extent the way in which the persona is presented (MARK; PEARSON, 2001) and the relationship established between those who encode and those who decode the messages (HALL, 2003) favours the understanding of these messages and motivates concrete actions, beyond the act of communication on the internet. The Curitiba City Hall Facebook page - nicknamed Pref's by users of this digital social network - is the persona of the master's thesis case study. The fanpage was selected because of its success since 2014 (with fans even among residents of other localities, who follow the posts and have made it have more followers than pages from capitals with larger populations). The posts, prepared and published by a multidisciplinary team, achieve significant numbers of interactions (KOOPMANS, 2004) with its users, even though there is no financial investment in Facebook advertising on the part of Curitiba City Hall. The main aim of this research is to present and analyse the implementation of actions proposed by the Pref's through the relationship established on digital social networks. The dissertation addresses the formation of the persona, the use of communication theories that have made it possible to reach a significant number of people through the propagation of messages (JENKINS; GREEN; FORD, 2014), as well as presenting case studies in which it is possible to verify the realisation of the actions. The corpus analysed involves posts that, during 2014 / 2015, required users not only to take action on the Internet itself, but also to put it into practice (such as making donations or taking part in social actions and awareness campaigns), thus establishing a communication and relationship process that goes beyond the "borders" of the Internet, apparently culminating in a rapprochement between citizens and the institution.

Keywords: Relationship. Digital Social Networks. Coding/Decoding. Resonance. Interaction.

SUMMARY

INTRODUCTION

During my professional development, understanding how to establish contact that minimises misunderstandings and provides a positive experience with customers has always been a question mark. Of all the experiences I've had in my career, which has ranged from counter clerk to telemarketer, salesperson, teacher and, more recently, entrepreneur, the customer service process has always been the one that has delighted and intrigued me the most[1] . In all the professions I've described above, customer service has always been present as a differentiating factor in the relationship between me (and my functions) and the customer I was dealing with.

One of the recurring concerns was that when we go to a restaurant where the food is excellent but the service is not commensurate with this excellence, it is the service experience that prevails and remains in our memory. However, if we go to a place where the food isn't a big difference, but the service experience is amazing, we'll keep that reference in our minds. When I chose to study for a master's degree, this concern motivated me to draw up a project that could give me a better understanding of the influences on an institutional relationship of service that is considered good by common sense. As communication has been present in my life due to my professional activity, looking for an object of study that would allow me to develop professionally, combined with personal development through research, became a challenge.

At first, I thought I would take a historical look at the entire communication process from the emergence of the Internet to social networks, not least because my first degree, in History, encouraged me to learn more about these concepts. As is common in the development of a dissertation, the definition of an object of study and the basis of the research gradually began to take shape. In the search for an object that could enable me to develop in various ways, finding something related to digital social networks proved to be the most viable option.

Thus, while observing the performance of various companies on the Internet, one institution caught my attention due to the great success it achieved with its Facebook page. It was the Curitiba City Council, through its fan page which won over fans all over Brazil with innovative and amusing posts that quickly turned it into a success story. I then chose to study this page, which apparently offered the possibility of combining my professional work on social networks with my concerns about the customer service process, since it was recognised that this City Hall page had thousands of fans due to its work. My object of study was thus defined.

The Curitiba City Hall Facebook page has become one of the best-known pages in Brazil due to the posts it publishes. Its acceptance was such that it even received the affectionate nickname Pref's (a name we'll explain in the course of the dissertation).

---

[1] I currently own a digital marketing agency which, among its many activities, develops actions and content for social networks. However, my professional development has been related to customer service, both through the company and through other experiences I've accumulated in my career, mainly as a call centre coordinator or as a history teacher, an activity I carried out for around 10 years.

Started in 2013 (BORBA, 2016), with the aim of opening up another channel of communication with Curitiba residents, the page gained more national exposure in 2014 due to the development of posts and messages that spread throughout Brazil, reaching fans far beyond the borders of the capital. This prominence enabled the city to reach hundreds of thousands of likes on its page, a number significantly higher than all of Brazil's capitals (including cities that have a larger population than Curitiba). All this success was due to a behaviour that until then had not been seen in the work of other capitals on this same channel, with posts reaching thousands of interactions (likes, comments and shares). What struck me most about this phenomenon was the fact that these posts suggested a relationship with their audience, through messages with content that seemed to be easily identified by those who followed them, but most of the time with an institutional message attached. It was by thinking about how these messages managed to achieve their institutional objectives that the problematic of my research was constructed.

It's important to point out that the Curitiba City Hall fanpage was taken offline in 2016 (when the master's work was finalised) due to issues related to the Electoral Law, more specifically Law 9.504/97, which establishes the rules for elections; however, this law does not explicitly prohibit the use of social networks by the City Hall, not least because the legislation predates the very existence of these digital social networks. The law states that public bodies cannot "authorise institutional advertising of the acts, programmes, works, services and campaigns of federal, state or municipal public bodies", except in cases of "serious and urgent public need". In order to update the legislation, a 2015 resolution by the Superior Electoral Court (TSE) ordered the suspension of these publications on the Internet during the election period. Thus, "Prefs" was taken down. According to the Prefecture's Internet and social media coordinator, Álvaro Borba (2016), each Pref's digital channel was taken offline according to the specifics of the social network in question[2] . Facebook, for example, offers an option to "freeze" the page - it continues to exist, but cannot be viewed by users (in the case of Twitter, all the content of the account linked to Pref's has been permanently deleted). With the end of the election period, the page tends to reappear with the same number of followers and an intact history.

There was a certain risk that the page would not resume its activity before the defence of this dissertation. For this reason, the content needed for the project was compiled (in print screen format) before the fanpage was taken offline. Even with the republishing of the page[3] , we preferred to keep the references that we had compiled, before the pause due to the electoral period, in the same format mentioned above.

In a digital communication process, more specifically on a social network, one of the main objectives is to talk to people, in other words, to open a communication "door" between a company/institution and its public (GABRIEL, 2010). In this way, we will address concepts such as interaction during the dissertation,

2 Based on an article published in the newspaper Paraná On-line. Available at: http://nrcm.net/prefsforadoar . Accessed on 30/07/2016

3 The website resumed its activities on 1 November 2016, after the end of the electoral period in the city of Curitiba.

which will appear in this research in two different contexts: the first concerns the relationship between an institution and people (those who need it, for example). In this approach, interaction has the meaning of participation and is therefore the realisation of the relationship between the two parties involved. The "idea of interaction also brings the practical dimension of an individual's actions" (FRANÇA; SIMÕES, 2015). For this research, this concept will be more relevant, as it is directly linked to the relationship.

The other interaction proposal that we will address during the research is related to the actions carried out by a person when in a digital social network environment. This involves liking, commenting on or sharing a post.

Among the various channels available to consolidate this process, Facebook deserves to be highlighted because, according to Ime Archibong[4] (2016), 8 out of 10 people who have access to the Internet in Brazil have an account on this social network. The relationships established on this digital channel make it possible for a company to talk to its public and also the other way round, i.e. for the public to interact with the company and also be noticed. However, I realised something in this process that was worth investigating. In particular, I wanted to analyse the extent to which the good relationship achieved by the town hall through its Facebook page made it possible for the communication process to take place in a concrete way. In other words, to what extent did the population that interacted with the page's posts actually recognise the institutional messages contained in the posts to the point of materialising actions related to the posts.

In this way, what this research aims to show is that even by achieving an intense and recognisably positive relationship with its public through Facebook, the City Council manages to establish a communication process that is assimilated by the people who follow it, culminating in the implementation of practical actions by its followers.

It is worth noting that in democratic societies, communication takes centre stage, as there is a need for access to information aimed at building citizenship. The very notion of citizenship, understood in a more active, participatory way, as the free exercise of rights and duties, only becomes possible when there is access to information (GARCIA, 2008). In this context, Lima (2010), based on the study of Aristotle's Politéia, states: "Being a citizen, in the sense of exercising citizenship, implies participation in one of the magistracies instituted in the polis. Citizens are all those who participate in the sovereign power that is fully exercised with a view to the well-being of the polis" (2010, p. 99).

To illustrate the implementation of actions, cases are presented that seem to have materialised as a result of a good relationship on a digital social network. This study then identifies real results, which have been accounted for not only by Pref's, but also by concrete actions, as well as local and national press coverage through their digital channels and even aired on television programmes.

The case study method used is a qualitative approach and is frequently used to collect data in the field

---

[4] Archibong is Director, **Strategic Partnerships** at Facebook. The reference is based on a talk he gave at Campus Party 2016. This same reference will be used again throughout the dissertation.

of organisational studies, despite the criticism levelled at it, considering that it lacks sufficient objectivity and rigour to be configured as a scientific research method. According to Yin (2001) and Fachin (2001), these issues can be present in other scientific research methods if the researcher does not have the training or skills necessary to carry out scientific studies; therefore, they are not inherent to the Case Study Method.

In addition to the case study, we also made the methodological choice of carrying out a literature review to provide a theoretical basis for understanding the actions carried out by Pref's.

In this research, we were able to define three theoretical bases that will guide us in the development of the dissertation. These are: The Encoding and Decoding model (HALL, 2003), the notion of Legitimacy, Visibility and Resonance (KOOPMANS, 2004) and Propagability (JENKINS; GREEN; FORD, 2014). Of these theories, Koppmans' (2004) is the one on which Pref's actions are based, as we were told in an interview by the person responsible for Pref's actions (BORBA, 2016). The others are proposed by the author of this dissertation to conceptually analyse the scenario.

Pref's emerged in 2013, in an attempt by the City Council to get closer to its audience and also to use the power of social networks to transmit matters related to the City Council, such as campaigns, social actions, information on the city's daily life, among others (BORBA, 2016). However, it was at the end of that same year, by creating bolder posts that tapped into the pop culture repertoire of the fanpage's followers, and by seeking to interact with the people who frequented the page, that the team in charge of the digital channels realised they could have greater freedom to create posts aimed at reaching a younger audience that recognised the symbols used to compose those messages. Thus, over the course of the following year, 2014, Pref's posts began to follow a pattern that ended up gaining thousands of followers. I therefore delimited the years 2014-2015 for the analyses, establishing the time frame of this project, as it was also in this same year that the Prefecture's fanpage gained national recognition, being singled out by newspapers, magazines and communication professionals as a highlight in the segment.

To develop the dissertation, we have organised the chapters as follows:

Chapter 01 - The emergence of Pref's: From the creation of the institutional website to the emergence of the relationship persona. In this chapter, we address issues related to an institution's need to position itself and relate digitally. Authors such as Gabriel (2010) and Martino (2014) helped us to understand how a social network is constituted. Finally, we present the concept of persona and the importance of establishing this concept in order to establish a position on social networks. Margaret Mark and Carol Pearson (2001) help us discuss this issue, presenting 12 archetypes for building a brand.

Chapter 02 - Message Development: Communication theories that are part of the Prefs' daily routine. Here the research focuses on the process of constructing a digital message. We use the definitions of Hall (2003), Jenkins, Green and Ford (2014) and Koopmans (2004) to understand in what context a message can be created to be replicated on digital social networks. Both authors offer concepts that enable a direct relationship with Pref's. In this chapter we also address the issue of repertoire; in other words, a message will have greater reach when it reaches the repertoire of the audience that follows a particular channel. We use some posts as examples to defend this idea.

Chapter 03 - More than a post: The use of Relationships as a form of digital communication - in this chapter we work on the concept of relationships associated with Relationship Marketing, a trend that has been taking hold in recent years, especially with the use of social networks. Mackenna (1993) and Peppers and Rogers (2004) contribute to this reflection. To show how important relationships are, even if they are fragile in contemporary times, we refer to Bauman (2004). Finally, Recuero (2009) helps us to understand the importance of interactions for the constitution of a digital relationship. Some more recent posts (after the time frame), which were selected with the aim of developing a scientific article on related topics, are also used as an example to illustrate the issues of interaction.

Finally, in *Chapter 04, The Realisation of Actions: case studies of actions developed by Pref's, we* analyse 3 campaigns developed on the page, campaigns which have given us data to understand the extent to which the communication process goes beyond the limits of the Internet, influencing practical life as well (and enabling actions to materialise outside the digital social network).

The first campaign we will use as a case study was one that had a huge impact, involving several cities through their fan pages. We're talking about the campaign that became known as Casamento Vermelho (Red Wedding), in which Curitiba City Hall and Rio de Janeiro City Hall decided to get married symbolically, inviting people to be godparents in this union; the suggested wedding gift was a mass blood donation. The campaign ended up generating positive developments, as companies took advantage of the situation to "gift" the city with various actions, ranging from painting themed graffiti to donating trainers to needy children.

The second campaign we analysed involved an action designed by Pref's to encourage bone marrow donation. It began when a citizen asked, via social media, for the support of Curitiba City Hall to publicise the urgent need for bone marrow donations to save a boy who liked superheroes; he was Enzo, who had Falconi's Anaemia (a disease that causes a type of leukaemia). The young man underwent two bone marrow transplants, but unfortunately passed away. To honour young Enzo, Pref's launched the Enzo Day campaign, which aimed to get as many people as possible to register to donate bone marrow. The campaign sensitised thousands of people and achieved significant results (especially for those who need this type of transplant).

The third action we analysed in this research is also related, in a way, to blood donation; it illustrates the reach that a digital social network can have and the speed at which information circulates on the Internet. In this campaign, Pref's publicised a call to find a person who was a blood donor and had a rare blood type. The need came from a city in Minas Gerais which, through the Paraná haemobank, requested that a certain person living in Curitiba (registered in the national database as a special donor) be found. Pref's joined in the search by publicising a call to find the person on its fan page. About 15 minutes after the publication, the person was found and it was possible to help save a life in Minas Gerais.

The choice of these actions, all of them related to health issues, was mainly due to the great sentimental appeal that the theme involves, noting that requests for blood and bone marrow donations are generally restricted to family circles who, in a time of need, spread the word among acquaintances to help a close person in need of such help. In this way, these actions will allow us to address the power of the reach established by Pref's relationship, as well as helping us to understand how this relationship, established between the fanpage and its audience, provides the realisation of a communication process.

CHAPTER 1

THE EMERGENCE OF PREFS: FROM THE CREATION OF THE INSTITUTIONAL WEBSITE TO THE EMERGENCE OF THE RELATIONSHIP PERSONA

Various events are part of a city's daily life. Issues related to health, education, security and other actions in a municipality are supposed to be brought to the attention of citizens so that they can interact with the day-to-day running of the municipality. The process of transmitting this type of information is undergoing a transformation due to the use of digital channels to propagate this type of information. In the recent past, in order to find out what was happening in a particular city, it was necessary to follow the media (such as printed newspapers, radio stations and, in the case of larger cities, television), as well as, of course, the possibility of travelling to the City Hall in person. Nowadays, especially since the advent of the Internet, these institutions have other channels such as websites and social networks where they can maintain closer contact with their citizens.

In this chapter we'll look at the creation of one of these digital channels by Curitiba City Hall, and how this process has contributed to establishing an image of the city that can be considered positive (which has led to recognition, including from local residents, for the actions carried out on social networks).

1.1 - INSTITUTIONS AND SOCIAL NETWORKS

Contemporary times have been presented and referred to as the information society.

> The demassification of civilisation, which reflects and intensifies the means of communication, brings with it a huge leap in the amount of information we all exchange with each other. And it is this increase that explains why we are becoming an 'information society'. (TOFFLER, 2014, p. 172)

We can say that the author's statement, even though it was developed in the 1980s (when the first edition of his work was published), is still valid, especially as technological innovations have become more accessible to people, thus contributing to this process gaining volume. Castells (1999) uses the term informationalism, a concept by which he describes technologies taking on a prominent role in all social segments, allowing us to understand the new social structure (network society) in which information technology is considered an indispensable tool in the manipulation of information and the construction of knowledge by individuals, since "the generation, processing and transmission of information becomes the main source of productivity and power" (CASTELLS, 1999, p.21).

It has been said that we live in a connected world, which presents us with possibilities for bringing people together through digital communication. The use of frequently appearing social networking channels allows people to connect through their affinities, or just by being part of a digital social network. The emergence of social networking platforms in the digital environment is a good example of how we are experiencing an era of greater information production. Many of the people who are part of these networks become potential content producers, making content of all types and formats available. All this information is created and shared with a view to building relationships between the parties that participate in a given channel.

But what does it mean to be part of a social network? In fact, these social networking environments did not emerge with the advent of technology: they have been part of human life for more than 3,000 years, ever since men sat around a campfire to talk and tell each other about their day (GABRIEL, 2010). What has changed in relation to the context in which we live in the 2010s is "the scope and spread of social networks as interactive communication technologies have developed" (GABRIEL, 2010, p. 193). The author is not referring specifically to the digital segment, but rather to technologies such as writing, postal services, telegraphs and, most recently, computers and the Internet. In this way, to be part of a social network is to be connected to other people, to relate to them through affinities, interests, leisure or information.

Primitive social networks, so to speak, were limited by various factors such as writing (since few people had the knowledge to read) and geography, which prevented people who were far away from each other from socialising. Today, with digital social networks, these barriers have been broken down by those who use them, to the extent that we can relate to people anywhere in the world. Even the writing barrier can be overcome if we consider that we have technology at our disposal that allows us to use audio and video resources to interact with people using these networks. Thus, according to Martha Gabriel (2010) "the essence of social networks is communication, and technologies are catalysing elements that facilitate interactions and communication sharing" (p. 194).

Nowadays there are various social networks for establishing relationships between people with common interests. As the digital communication market grows, new possibilities for interaction arise based on market niches, so that people are linked to a particular network based on their affinity with the subjects dealt with in that space. Even with the diversity of channels and segments, one of these digital social networks is the one that has generated the most attention, as millions of people around the world are part of it. We're talking about Facebook. Up until now, in 2016, no virtual social network had such a significant reach as this one. It is possible to make this statement considering that of the 40% of the population who have access to the Internet, more than 1/3 have a Facebook account[5] ; in other words, 1 in 3 people who have access to the Internet use this channel in some way to socialise, share information, photos, videos and any content they deem relevant. This is precisely the point that makes it relevant, because content created for other digital channels such as blogs and corporate websites can also be shared on Facebook, so that your friends can interact with these posts, which significantly increases the reach of this content.

"This Network is a complex communication structure in which several nodes interact" (MARTINO,

---

[5] Facebook beats analysts' revenue estimates; users now number 1.4bn. Available at http://www1.folha.uol.com.br/tec/2015/01/1581963-facebook-supera-estimativa-de-receita-de-analistas-usuarios-ja- sao-14-bi.shtml Accessed on 29/05/2015

2014, p. 100). In his book Digital Media Theory, Martino (2014) describes that in a social network "each person is a node. Each page or community, in turn, is another node, and finally, a social network site is the node of nodes" (MARTINO, 2014, p.100). Based on this statement, we can say that social networks have become a great agglutinator of people. Thus, using these networks is a way of communicating with individuals, reaching more and more nodes and, consequently, spreading information even further.

However, these channels are not specifically for communication between people; they have also been used by institutions as a way of getting closer to their public and thus establishing a relationship. For this research, it is important to define what is considered a relationship. To do this, we will use the concepts of Peppers and Rogers (2004) who approach the subject by defining that

> a relationship implies reciprocity. For any 'state of affairs' to be considered a relationship, both parties have to participate and be aware of the existence of the relationship. This means that relationships must inherently be two-way in nature. This may seem like common sense. You can't have a relationship with another person if they don't have a relationship with you (2004, p. 36).

When we talk about an institutional action for a company to get closer to its public, we are referring to the concept of Relationship Marketing. Mackenna (1993) suggests that this type of marketing presupposes interaction and connection between consumers and companies, so that the former can participate in the process of organising and planning products and services for the latter. These concepts will be covered and discussed again in chapter 3 of this research, when we will then show in more detail the relationship between this theme and this dissertation.

Relationships are a key concept for this research, mainly because it is through them that a public institution has been communicating with its public. The institution in question is the Curitiba City Council which, through an official Facebook page created to relate to its citizens, has achieved significant results in terms of reaching its public, thus establishing a relationship between the parties. However, as mentioned, for there to be a relationship between an institution (or company) and the people who follow it, there needs to be interaction between them.

Some authors present concepts that contribute to understanding what interaction means, an understanding that will accompany us throughout this dissertation. Alex Primo (2007) tackles the subject, directing his concept towards the social environment: "social interaction is characterised not only by the messages exchanged (the content) and by the interactants who meet in a given context (geographical, social, political, temporal), but also by the relationship that exists between them" (p.7). The author also points out a difference between interaction and communication that we think is important to emphasise: "Understanding that interaction is 'action between' and communication is 'shared action', we want to study what happens between the participants in the interaction, here called interactants" (PRIMO, 2007, p. 56). The idea of interaction also brings the practical dimension of an individual's action, which is driven by the orientation of the other. França and Simões (2015) argue that an interaction involves "a joint, shared, reciprocally referenced action: an inter-action" (p. 168). The concept thus designates a situation in which not only do the actors interact, but they also define the framework of the action and the meaning of the interaction. Goffman (2002) defines interaction as the mutual influence of individuals on each other's behaviour in a given situation and it is the multiple interactions in which they engage that constitute social life.

Organisations today tend to look for new ways of building relationships with their audiences in order to build loyalty and insert them into a climate of collaborative interaction in the construction of products and the propagation of brands through digital social networks. This need is no different in a public institution like Curitiba City Hall. The search for a relationship with a city's public is one of the challenges of public communication. Simply informing citizens of what's happening in a city is not enough. It is also necessary to encourage participation through the same communication process.

> Public communication, then, must be understood in a broader sense than just providing information. It must include the possibility for citizens to be fully aware of the information that concerns them, including that which they don't seek out because they don't know it exists, the possibility of expressing their positions with the certainty that they will be listened to with interest and the prospect of actively participating, of obtaining guidance, education and dialogue. (DUARTE, 2007, p.64)

The consolidation of this new format of public communication is in line with what has been called e-participation[6] (SAMPAIO, 2013); or even Digital Democracy, which can be defined in this way:

> I understand digital democracy to mean any form of use of devices (computers, mobile phones, smartphones, palmtops, ipads...), applications (programmes) and tools (forums, websites, social networks, social media...) of digital communication technologies to supplement, reinforce or correct aspects of the political and social practices of the state and citizens for the benefit of the democratic content of the political community (GOMES, 2011, p. 27-28).

This concept is complemented by Sampaio (2013) when he states:

> the concept of Digital Democracy, in our view, is linked to the idea of different uses of the Internet by citizens, civil society actors and the formal political class, which can strengthen, encourage or foster different democratic values at different levels.(2013, p.60)

The communication technologies available make it possible to expose social, political, economic and cultural problems, as well as living with the new, the diverse and discovering different ways of dealing with them. From this scenario, partial public spaces can emerge, free from an institutionalised political conception. "In this virtual space, networks of debates are established, by area of interest or knowledge, which produce and reproduce meanings, articulate, negotiate and legitimise the thematic diversity, values, needs and conflicts of the offline world[7] " (GUEDES, 2010, p.12). Wolton (2003), presenting a logic of mass democracy,

---

[6] The letter "e" refers to "electronic" and comes before the noun to be named (participation).

[7] The author makes a distinction in her article between the offline and online (virtual) worlds, but we don't agree with this concept. For this research, we will consider the virtual to be an extension of the so-called offline world, in other words, they are a continuum. This concept is worked on by Daniel Miller, co-authored with

understands the public space as "[...] with a far greater number of actors intervening in a public way, an omnipresence of information, polls, marketing and communication" (p.199). This space also refers to subjects who are capable of building their own opinions, who recognise others and believe in the power of argumentation, thus requiring time to form.

Even though there are differing opinions about who is part of this public space, we believe that the point of convergence is currently represented by the characters, whether they are from the elite or the people, because they contribute to the development of institutions through information; in other words, by taking part in the process of propagating[8] information and, often, why not, creating situations in which they no longer become passive, but rather important players in relation to what happens in the public sphere. In the case of Curitiba City Hall, by opening up its Facebook channel, it has also opened up a possibility for conversation and interaction with its public that, if compared to traditional media, would not be as comprehensive as in the digital environment. Being able to participate in a public issue from the comfort of your own home, through comments and shares on a social network, allows for a greater number of interactions compared to those where it is necessary to be present. Even though there are other channels (telephone and physical), the agility of a social network shows that innovation is needed to meet this new demand. This innovation is necessary because it is necessary to attract the attention of the public that uses a digital social network like Facebook. For a post to reach a number of interactions, the content of the message must provoke an action (like, comment or share) from those who follow that channel.

If the idea is to find new ways of building relationships, public institutions (such as Curitiba City Hall) have had to look for alternatives that favour bringing institutions and their public closer together. We are experiencing a media transformation that

> reached its apex when the individual realised that instead of being exposed to messages from a single receptive device such as television, in which he only received the messages, he could have access to various portable technologies such as mobile phones and mobile computers, which not only allow him to receive messages but also to produce content and share it with his network of friends. (GONÇALVES, 2015 p.122)

In this way, those who want to reach a certain audience must speak the same language as them. In other words, it is necessary to establish a kind of repertoire synchronisation in which the receiver of the message recognises and identifies with the content of that particular publication (NETTO, 1996). One of the alternatives for making this possible is to use marketing strategies so that there is an institutional identity without this strategy affecting the language established (and recognised) by users within a given network. In the case of Facebook, due to technical issues that limit the exposure of institutional pages (companies,

---

Don Slater (2004), who discusses the continuity between the online and offline worlds in a study carried out in Internet cafés in Trinidad.

[8] The term propagation is related to propagability, a theoretical concept that will be addressed later in this dissertation from the perspective of (JENKINS; GREEN; FORD, 2014).

institutions, public figures) on that network, it is worth explaining how this process works.

Many of the users who are part of the Facebook social network use the channel with the aim of socialising through photos, text posts and videos. Each person creates their own personal profile and tries to connect with other people on the network. Once this communication has been established, the user starts to see posts made by the people with whom they have established a connection on their screen, known as their timeline. The social network's algorithm establishes that in order for you to see what is happening with your "friends", there must be an interaction (like, comment or share); in this way, Facebook's algorithm identifies which friends interact with you the most (and vice versa), thus establishing a ranking of posts to be displayed on the user's timeline. This algorithm is known as EdgeRank (WHAT IT IS, 2016). Through this index, each post that is published receives a score that will determine its degree of exposure. If the score is low, few people will see it. Conversely, if the score is high, the greater the distribution of the post and, consequently, the greater the prominence given to it. Therefore, it is this calculation that determines, based on the relationship that has taken place on the network, which post should appear on people's timelines.

Facebook also offers the possibility for companies (legal entities) to create an official page, known as a fanpage, so that people can interact with a brand, product, service or even people, if we consider artists who take on an institutional role on the network to be a legal entity (POR QUE É, 2016). Just as an illustrative example, a particular artist can have a personal profile (individual) where they interact with friends in an intimate way and also a Fanpage (legal entity) where they open a channel of communication with their fans.

Even though this possibility has been developed for companies, Facebook's premise is for (natural) people to connect, so posts between these types of profiles are favoured. Facebook's algorithm restricts the reach that posts made by fan pages have on private profiles. For these pages, EdgeRank is even more important, because it is only through effective relationships that the posts made by the organisations will have a greater audience reach. To complement this scenario, if this relationship is not established between institutions and personal profiles, it is through investment and media, i.e. buying advertising space (on Facebook) that it will be possible to reach a greater number of people (QUANDO VALE, 2016).

But what is the best way to reach people and get them to interact with a particular page, thus guaranteeing good post positioning? To answer this question, digital marketing professionals use different strategies, such as posting at certain times (trying to be present at times when the largest number of users are using the social network), identifying a target audience, using posts that are recognised as successful on the network (photos of animals, memes[9] , viral videos), all with the aim of attracting the public's attention. One of these strategies, which is part of the daily routine of professionals working in this area, is the creation of a Persona.

---

[9] **Memes** are posts, mostly images, that aim to convey an idea. The term was coined by Dawkins (2007) who defined it as a unit of information (idea or behaviour) that is transmitted from brain to brain.

1.2 - CREATING THE PREF'S PERSONA

The concept of persona adopted in this work comes from psychology, more specifically from Carl Gustav Jung (2008). The author, in a study of what he calls the collective unconscious, develops this concept as one of the archetypes of human personality. An archetype can be understood as an inherited pattern of behaviour or emotion. Its nature is such that we recognise it instantly and are able to attribute a specific emotional meaning to it. The persona, in turn, includes our social roles, the type of clothes we choose to wear and our style of personal expression. The term "persona" is derived from the Latin word for mask, which refers to the masks worn by actors in Greek drama to give meaning to the roles they were playing. The words "person" and "personality" are also related to this term.

> As its name reveals, it is simply a mask of the collective psyche, a mask that appears to be an individuality, trying to convince others and itself that it is an individuality, when in reality it is nothing more than a role in which the collective psyche speaks. (JUNG, 2008, pg.43)

The persona has both positive and negative aspects. A dominant persona can stifle the individual and those who identify with their persona tend to see themselves only in the superficial terms of their social roles and façade. Jung (2008) also called the persona the "archetype of conformity", because the posture of a persona is appropriate in every social context experienced. However, the persona serves to protect the ego[10] and the psyche[11] from the various social forces and attitudes that invade us. It is also considered an instrument for communication, since it can play an important role in our positive development as we begin to act in a certain way, playing a role, thus allowing our ego to gradually adapt in the direction of the persona created.

These concepts, applied to understanding human beings, have been used as a digital communication strategy, especially in work related to social networks. In order for people who interact with a particular page to be able to recognise and identify with that page, the concept of the Brand Persona is used[12] (MARK; PEARSON, 2001).

The aim of creating a brand persona is to give institutions (legal entities) a human character and establish a virtual personality. In this way, it is possible to get closer to your audience without this necessarily meaning that there is a commercial relationship between the parties. By creating a brand persona, the brand is represented and consequently perceived by the public in a more spontaneous and informal way. This process was often used in advertising even before the advent of the Internet, as a way of bringing brands (products and

---

[10] The Ego: is your notion of individuality, how you perceive yourself, according to your experiences through your culture, the education you received and your physical body (Book of Psychology, 2012, p.95).

[11] The psyche, according to Freud, resembles an iceberg, with areas of primitive drives, the id, hidden in the unconscious, the Ego that deals with conscious thought and the super-ego, which is the critical and judgemental voice (Book of Psychology, 2012, p.96).

[12] We'll use the term brand to exemplify this concept, since the same company can have several brands associated with it; however, each one will probably have an individual persona.

services) closer to their consumer audience. Digital channels have appropriated this concept as a way of strengthening relations between pages (websites, fanpages, YouTube channels) and their followers.

Recuero (2009) points out: "Social networking sites were defined by Boyd & Ellison (2007) as those systems that allow (i) the construction of a persona through a profile or personal page; (ii) interaction through comments; and (iii) the public exposure of each actor's social network" (p. 102). In this way, we can understand that building a persona is necessary for brands that want to be on the web and thus interact, share and exchange content with their respective audiences. The main aim of personifying brands is to engage[13] with their followers. By taking on a role, the organisation detaches itself from an unattainable and rigid image and starts to be seen as "human", since it is given a personality.

Before social networks, companies generally just displayed their products, trying to stand out because of price, some kind of exclusivity or market positioning. It was very difficult for a person to interact directly with the brand, to talk to it. Even though customer service departments such as SACs (customer service centres) were available to the public, the dynamics of the conversation process were one-sided. In other words, the consumer contacted the brand to clarify doubts, make suggestions or complaints; they were listened to, their request was answered and, after this process, the relationship between them was closed. A new interaction required a new call and a new demand. This process worked well (to a certain extent it still does) with private institutions; but in public organisations such as a town hall[14] , the same result was not always achieved. With social media, brands are now offering a process of constant, two-way interaction, in which information is made available and people can interact with it. In this sense, we can better understand this process of exchange if we consider the platforms as a relational intermediary space, in which:

> The contemporary consumer inhabits, but also public or private institutions, communities, society in all its dimensions - political, economic, technological, legal and cultural - in which the public and the private, the collective and the individual, necessarily exchange far beyond the dimensions of space and time, making use of multidirectional flows, seeing and being seen, changing and being changed. (GALINDO, 2013, p.60)

As this space is relational, it's up to the brand to interact with its public all the time, listening to their needs and expectations. To operate on the web, you need to build collaborative environments so that customers feel engaged. The need for a relationship with the public on a social network is a major trend in corporate communication, which expresses itself in the world of digital networks by creating a presence in new territories with their respective publics.

---

[13] Engagement refers to the interactions that people have with each post published on a social network. In the case of Facebook, this engagement is measured by likes, comments and shares of a given post.

[14] In addition to the physical service, Curitiba City Hall offers a call centre, 156, where the population can get in touch with various complaints, doubts, denunciations, among other possible requests. The service, however, receives a lot of criticism due to the difficulty in getting through to an agent. (Paraná On-Line. Available at : http://www.tribunapr.com.br/noticias/parana/populacao-reclama-de-demora-nos-servicos-publicos/ accessed on 08/08/2016)

The creation of a persona is therefore part of a strategy by institutions or brands seeking to get closer to their audience. This importance is emphasised by Sandra Turchi (2013) when she says:

> One of the main strategies for this humanisation is the creation of what we call a Brand Persona, which should be discussed even before defining your logo. This persona takes into account your history, emotional and physical characteristics, personality, values and ideas that are compatible with those of your target audience, which may change over time as you experience and learn new things (online).

Thus, the proposal to create a persona arises from the need to get closer to your audience in a more effective way, so that those who follow the day-to-day running of a company can not only admire the brand, but also be part of its actions.

Using this study of personas as a basis, digital communication strategies have worked to create an identification process with their target audience that allows the brand to talk directly to those who follow it. By taking on this role, companies are able to create their own personality and be recognised for it; in other words, their positioning, through a persona, is what will attract a certain audience to digital channels, such as social networks for example. On these channels, creating a persona is an important part of the communication process, since a large volume of information available on the web, creating an identification with your audience can be decisive in gaining greater adherence to published content, thus helping the message reach an even greater number of people.

To perfect this process of creating a persona for a brand, Margaret Mark and Carol Pearson (2001), in their book "The Hero and the Outlaw", created 12 archetypes (based on the theory proposed by Jung) that contribute to defining a persona for brands seeking a relationship with their public. To better understand the meaning of each of these archetypes (and how we can relate them to our object of study), we will briefly describe each one below.

Let's start with the Creator archetype. When the Creator archetype is active in individuals, they feel compelled to create or innovate - otherwise they suffocate. Any artistic activity is useful in satisfying the desire for harmony and stability, as well as raising the individual's self-esteem. In terms of its use as a marketing tool, this archetype also provides an evocation of status to its products. Many expensive products, such as property, sculptures and carpets are negotiated using the Creator archetype (2001, p.235).

Then there's the Prestative. This is someone who is altruistic, driven by compassion, generosity and the desire to help others. They fear instability and difficulty, not so much for themselves, but for the impact on people who are less fortunate or less resistant to shocks. It is perceived in activities related to the provision of services, both to individuals and to organisations and corporations (2001, p.217).

The Ruler is always in charge and in control. It is typical to be shown as an extremely responsible individual who fulfils many important responsibilities. Products and services related to the archetype reaffirm the power, prestige and status of the client or consumer. They are generally related to class "A" audiences" (2001, p.251).

When the court jester archetype is active in a persona, they just want to have fun. The basic desire here is to be spontaneous and recapture that playful spirit we all had when we were little (2001, p.203).

The Common Face is represented by a language that is colloquial and opposed to any kind of elitism. The aim of this archetype is to be part of the group and equal to everyone (2001, p.171).

The Lover wants a deeper kind of connection: one that is intimate, genuine and personal. It's common in the cosmetics, jewellery, fashion and tourism industries (2001, p.185).

When the Hero archetype is active in a persona, they are strengthened by the challenge, feel outraged by injustice and respond quickly and decisively to the crisis or opportunity. It can be used in marketing linked to social causes, such as social marketing itself - which seeks to influence the behaviour of a certain target audience, with a view to the greater well-being of society in the long term (2001, p.113).

The Outlaw archetype is also known as the revolutionary. It unleashes the repressed passions of society. When the consciousness of the Outlaw is present, people have a more acute perception of the limits that civilisation imposes on human expression (2001, p.131).

The Magician represents the archetype of those who wish to seek out the essential principles that govern how things work and use them to make things happen. They are motivated by the desire for personal transformation and the opportunity to change people, organisations and the times (2001, p.147).

When the Innocent is active in a persona, they are drawn to certainty, to positive and hopeful ideas, to simple and nostalgic images, to the promise of rescue and redemption (2001, p.63).

In the Explorer archetype, his call is to explore the world and, in the process, to find himself in order to know who he is (2001, p.79).

Finally, the Wise One, who, when active in a person's life, is keenly interested in learning for learning's sake. From this definition, it is possible to conclude that when the archetype of the Sage predominates in an individual's character, there is great and constant motivation and interest in learning (2001, p.95).

The authors have grouped these 12 archetypes into 4 main groups: (i) Mastery/Risk - when we want to do something remarkable and be remembered forever and when we fight for our dreams. Even if it means breaking rules and overcoming challenges. This group includes the Hero, Outlaw and Magician archetypes; (ii) Independence/Satisfaction: realised when there is a desire to be alone, reflect, decide and get to know the real me. In this division we find the archetypes of the Innocent, Explorer and Sage; (iii) Belonging/Pleasure: in this sector we find situations in which the person feels a deep need to belong to a group. Characteristic here are the archetypes of the Court Fool, Common Face and Lover; (iv) Stability/Control: perceived when we want to have a certain control over things, a power in our hands, characteristics which are perceived in the archetypes of the Creator, Provider and Ruler (MARK; PEARSON, 2001, p. 31). Below is a table (table 1) with the organisation of these groups to better illustrate the concept described by the authors.

Archetypes			
Mastery / Risk	**Independence / Satisfaction**	**Belonging / Pleasure**	**Stability / Control**
Hero	Innocent	Court jester	Creator

Outlaw	Explorer	Ordinary Face	Helpful
Magician	Wise	Lover	Ruler

Table 1- Organisation of Archetypes
source: organised by the author, based on (MARK; PEARSON, 2001, p. 31)

The study by Mark and Pearson (2001) points to the importance of defining a persona so that a brand can interact more closely with its audience, suggesting that this proximity provides results in terms of the reach that a given publication can have. On social networks, reach is something of significant importance, as it indicates the number of people who have viewed this or that message. When we're talking about a public institution, one of whose duties is to inform its citizens, having a good reach can mean talking to more people.

Many of these institutions have ended up adopting digital tools, such as Facebook, to get closer to their public. As mentioned earlier, this social network absorbs a large proportion of active internet users.

Curitiba City Hall was no different. Creating a fanpage became a necessity, especially when it was confirmed that the city would be one of the hosts of the football World Cup, which took place in Brazil in 2014. Aiming to provide yet another channel for interaction with its public, in 2013 a team multidisciplinary team was created to "take care" of the City Hall's social network. According to Álvaro Borba, director of the City Hall's Internet and social media department,

> In 2013, the management of Curitiba City Hall opened its work promising to recapture the innovative character for which the city had become known in the past, with the adoption of unprecedented solutions in various departments. The willingness to innovate created space for cheap and innovative ideas to be presented. Each area contributed in its own way. The Social Communication Department's collaboration was the creation of the Internet and Social Media Department (2016).

The premise behind the formation of this department was to establish a rapprochement with citizens in a cheaper way, taking advantage of the viralisation potential that a social network can offer. In addition to the reach possible with actions on this channel, an objective to be fulfilled by this team was to reach as many people as possible at the lowest possible advertising investment cost. As already mentioned, when it comes to Facebook, establishing a connection with your audience effectively, i.e. when people actually interact with the page through likes, shares and comments, can help messages reach a greater number of people. If these interactions don't occur, the alternative is to invest in advertising on the network itself to reach a significant number of network users. The City Council invests millions[15] of reais in institutional advertising to propagate its campaigns in the different sectors that make it up; thus, the creation of the fanpage "uses the viralisation potential of the networks in which we operate and we direct all our creative effort so that the phenomenon of viralisation acts on our institutional messages" (BORBA, 2016).

[15] This statement takes into account the bidding process opened by the City Council in 2014 to hire advertising agencies, which was expected to cost R$20 million that year. This contract was suspended by the Paraná Court of Auditors (TC-PR) as reported in the newspaper Gazeta do Povo Available at: http://www.gazetadopovo.com.br/vida-publica/Prefeitura-de-curitiba-suspende-licitacao-de-publicidade- por-ordem-do-tc-evjinb7ea3zs69v8outffnb66 Accessed on 07/05/2016

However, in order for these objectives to be achieved, it was necessary for the professionals in charge of the department to create the persona of this fanpage so that it could identify with its audience. Elizabeth Moraes Gonçalves (2015) describes the importance of this approach when she says:

> The network society only subsists through collaboration and in order to stay alive in this society it is necessary to interact with its audiences, to create communication strategies that are no longer aimed at the masses, but at the individual consumer, who, by feeling part of the process, will be able to respond as a communication agent and disseminate content through their network of friends, in favour of the brand (p. 123).

So the team developed a persona that tries to counteract the stereotype of Curitiba's inhabitants, which according to Borba, "is that of a grumpy, closed-off person" (2016). A receptive and humorous personality is created, in an attempt to work on this negative perception and make the local community realise their true values, and so "Pref's" emerges. According to Borba, in an informal conversation during the contact made by the author of this dissertation with the team, the expression Pref's was created by one of the followers of the fanpage, and came to be adopted internally by the team as a way of referring to the Facebook page. Once the institution's personality was defined on the web, it began to act as a bridge between citizens and the events taking place in the city. For this to happen, the team then created three categories of content: "service (what the City Hall offers), education (messages that guide citizens in exercising their individuality) and citizenship (messages that guide citizens on how to contribute to the collective)" (BORBA, 2016).

If we use the archetypes described by Mark & Pearson (2001) as a reference, we can relate Pref's persona to the archetypes Prestativo (since one of the social functions of the website is to contribute to the development of the city through the information provided, thus categorising it as a service) and Bobo da Corte (since brands that adopt this archetype as one of their personalities have the basic desire to "live in the present moment, with total joy" (p.204)).

To establish this format of interaction, two posts were highlighted by the team as those that contributed to defining the Pref's persona. Before mentioning these posts, it's worth emphasising that the City Council's presence on the web goes beyond its Facebook page. Other channels, such as Twitter, Instagram and most recently Snapchat[16] , are part of Pref's assumed persona. The reason for this is because the first post that contributed to the formation of this persona was initially published on Twitter and later replicated on Facebook.

The aim of this post was to publicise an event, the so-called Cultural Current[17] , which takes place annually in the capital of Paraná. To this end, Pref's published a
image (figure 1) telling a story about a giant capybara that would invade the city. We believe that the use of a

---

[16] Social network, through a smartphone application in which photo or video content is available for a fixed period of time (maximum 24 hours). More information can be found on the app's portal: https ://www. snapchat. com/l/en-br/brand-guidelines

[17] Corrente Cultural is a union of various cultural promoters in Curitiba who come together to offer an intense cultural programme for the city over the course of a week. Corrente Cultural is organised by the Curitiba Cultural Foundation (FCC) and the Curitiba Institute of Art and Culture (ICAC). Available at: www.correntecultural.com.br/oquee Accessed on 07/05/2016.

capybara was due to the fact that these animals are often seen in city parks. So its use in the post, even in an exaggerated and unusual way, may have been published with the aim of attracting people's attention. This is an obvious use of the court jester archetype.

Figure 1 - Post Capivara Gigante / Corrente Cultural Source: Curitiba City Hall Twitter account

> The post was so successful that the capybara became a local mascot. Today, Curitiba's Pro-Citizenship Institute has a product line based on the capybara. The funds raised finance the work of Curitiba's Social Action Foundation (BORBA, 2016).

In fact, the post was such a success that the team felt the need to continue the action as a way of interacting with the users who had shown up on the networks where the image had been posted. So a second image (figure 2), in reference to the first one, was published to maintain the positive atmosphere, since it maintained the joking aspect with the image of the capybara, also reaching a significant number of people. Once again we see the court jester archetype in a Pref's message.

Prefeitura Curitiba @Curitiba_PMC · 7 de nov de 2013
Tranquilizamos todos os cidadãos avisando que essa imagem, publicada recentemente no instagram, não é real. Obrigado.

Figure 2 Image in response to the good repercussions of the giant capybara post.
Source: Curitiba City Hall Twitter account

About a month after this episode, a new post contributed to the consolidation of Pref's persona. A post aimed at warning citizens about a storm approaching the city had, among the many comments, a comment that caught the team's attention, thus creating an interaction with its followers that would come to symbolise the language with which Pref's would communicate with its public. The image posted (figure 3) to warn about the storm was of one of the city's buildings which, because it was under construction, had safety nets flying off in the wind.

Figure 3 Image published as a warning of approaching storms.
Source: Curitiba City Hall Fanpage

Among the many comments made on this post, one stood out because of its unusual nature. The comment was simple: "Dementors :O[18] " (figure 4).

Dementors are characters from the Harry Potter film series (figure 5). In the film sequence, the young wizard and main character of the franchise fights these beings by applying a spell called the "Patronum spell", which consists of summoning an animal to fight the dementors. So, as a way of interacting with this single comment, Pref's launches a new post, this time with a Patronum spell, using one of the city's tourist attractions, "The Drooling Horse"[19] (figure 6).

---

[18] The comment was accompanied by a symbol commonly used on social networks, the so-called emoticons, which are drawings of faces symbolising human expressions. In this case, the emoticon symbolised a surprised face.

[19] The famous sculpture of the horse that lets water out of its mouth (figure 7), located in Largo da Ordem, is a tribute to the muleteers who left the countryside for Curitiba in the 20th century and left their horses hitched up in the city centre, where the capital's biggest shopping centres were located. Available at: http://curitibacultcom.br/o-cavalo-babao-largo-da-ordem-historia-e-lenda-urbana-por-tras-monument/ Accessed on 19/08/2016.

Figura 5- Dementadores – Harry Potter
Fonte: Google Imagens

Figura 4 – Print de tela com o comentário: Dementadores :O
Fonte: Fanpage da Prefeitura Municipal de Curitiba

Figure 4 - Screenshot with the comment: Dementadores :O Source: Curitiba City Hall Fanpage

Figure 5- Dementors - Harry Potter Source: Google Images

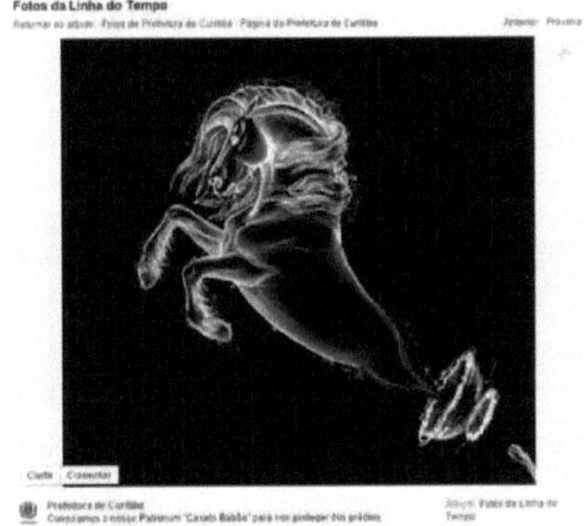

Figura 7 - Escultura em homenagem aos tropeiros. "Cavalo babão"

Figura 6 – Post "Patronum Cavalo Babão"

Figure 6 - "Patronum Cavalo Babão" post

Figure 7 - Sculpture in honour of the muleteers. "Drooling horse"

From these posts, the language adopted by the team would then follow a more stripped-down, cheerful and informal character perceived in the archetype of the court jester, whose goal is to have fun and make the world happy (MARK; PERSON, 2001, p. 204). A number of posts that could be considered amusing and unusual took over the web, allowing Pref's to reach a significant number of people. The interesting thing about this process is that these posts, although full of humour, always have some institutional information attached to the message. These aren't just funny posts, but messages from an institution aimed at reaching its audience.

Over time, the Pref's fan page has gained prominence not only among Curitiba residents, but also among people in various cities throughout Brazil. The relationship gained with this audience went beyond empathising with the post itself; the Pref's persona may have changed the way people perceive the city of

Curitiba. Traditionally, its inhabitants have been labelled as closed-minded, soft-spoken and difficult to get along with. As the persona created took over digital social networks and won over the public, the image of the city's residents also changed. One way of observing this change is with the publication of an article in the magazine Exame[20] which named Curitiba as the funniest capital in the country. In addition to this, other media outlets also reported on the success achieved on the networks, publishing headlines such as "How Curitiba City Hall maintains the best Facebook page"[21] and "Curitiba City Hall uses humour on Facebook and wins fans[22] . This news helped the city gain national and international prominence, as happened in the 1990s when the city was awarded the title of "Model City[23] ".

This recognition attracted people's attention to the city (which already had a good reputation) but created an identity in which the city is represented by the Pref's Persona. In many of the comments on these posts, people say they want to get to know this Curitiba, they want to interact with a city that they know virtually, but believe has the same personality as on social media.

These actions seem to demonstrate the "power" that creating a persona can have for an institution. Contributing to a process of re-signifying the image of an entire city is not a simple task, but according to those who are part of the team, it was never the real objective of creating this personality. Given that many of the residents, even though they like the fan page and the funny posts, have not changed their image of the city, but interact with the institution in a freer and more open way, apparently trying to follow the same model proposed by the persona.

In order to symbolise the whole process devised by the team behind the Pref's persona, we will now transcribe a text they published on their page which, according to those responsible, reflects the reasons why Pref's is what it is on the networks. The context in which this text was published refers to a response given by the team, or rather the persona, to the São Paulo City Council, which criticised Pref's approach to social media. When asked by one of their followers why they didn't adopt the same language as the capital of Paraná, the team in charge of the São Paulo fanpage explained the reason for their conduct, and criticised the persona created by the Curitiba team, saying that they make "virtual perfumery" (figure 8).In response to this context, Pref's published the following text:

> Curitiba is determined to be an increasingly humane city. Within our possibilities, all our

[20] Exame magazine article: Curitiba is now the funniest city in Brazil; see why. Available at: http://exame.abril.com.br/brasil/noticias/curitiba-e-hoje-cidade-mais-engracada-do-brasil-veja-razao Accessed on 28/04/2016.

[21] How Curitiba City Hall maintains the best Facebook page. Available at: http://www.digai.com.br/2014/08/como-Prefeitura-de-curitiba-mantem-melhor-pagma-facebook/ Accessed on 28/04/2016.

[22] Curitiba City Hall uses humour on Facebook and wins fans. Available at: http://noticias.terra.com.br/brasil/cidades/Prefeitura-de-curitiba-usa-humor-no-facebook-e-ganha-fas.1042b5ae60a65410VgnVCM3000009af154d0RCRD.html Accessed on 28/04/2016.

[23] In an interview with The Wall Street Journal in 1992, the then president of the World Bank, Michael Cohen, said that Curitiba was a model city for the First World, not just for the Third. This quote appears in Aline Albuquerque's master's thesis (2007).

> actions are aligned with
> for this purpose, including communication. We see social networks as a very important tool for achieving this goal. Our endeavour is to ensure that all citizens who come to us are heard. For this to happen, we need to adopt the same attitude to praise as to criticism: one of gratitude - thank you! We have good reason to believe that online interactions can make the offline world a better place. We've seen this happen on several occasions: by interacting with Prefs, you've mobilised for blood drives, book collections, social actions, etc. Interacting with Prefs, you've done so many beautiful things that it's hard to list - thank you again! All of this was only possible because Prefs was humble enough to accept the language and aesthetics that dominate social networks. We understand that it is the public authorities that should endeavour to get closer to people, not the other way around. That's how the Prefecture became the Prefs; a nickname you gave us and we accepted - and we can't stop thanking you: thank you! There are those among scholars and communication professionals who turn up their noses at the memes you share here. There are those who believe that this is a shallow and silly form of communication, without the potential to convey complex messages. We respect their opinion, but we base our work on another perception: memes are entertainment made by millions and consumed by millions. Memes are also popular culture and should be understood as such, without prejudice. Prefs agrees to approach this popular culture whenever it can fulfil one of these three objectives: to publicise services, to educate and to promote citizenship. Using this language already makes Curitiba see itself in a different light. The city, which used to see itself as bad-tempered, is beginning to have a different relationship with its identity. And that's great! If we believe that we are bad-tempered and unwilling to get along with each other and accept this as an unchangeable reality, we won't be able to build the humane city that we dream of (Curitiba City Hall Fanpage, 2015).[24]

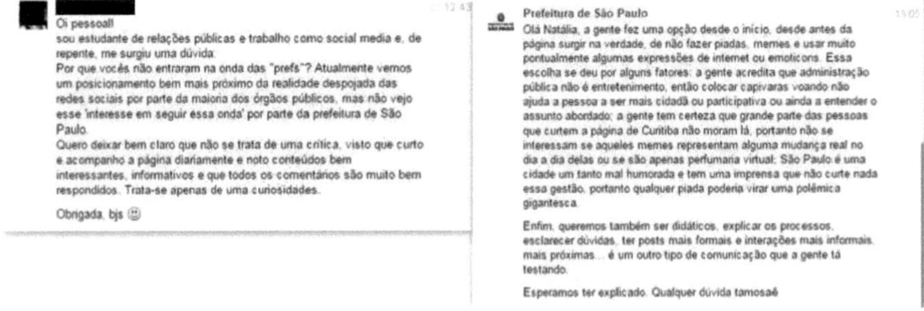

Figure 8 - Screenshot of the conversation between the internet user and São Paulo City Hall on Facebook
Source: Gazeta do Povo online. Available at: http://www.gazetadopovo.com.br/vida-publica/Prefeitura-de-sao- paulo-diz-que-curitiba-faz-perfumaria-no-facebook-3xqvoe0 Accessed on 28/04/2016

This text literally translates the thinking and attitude of the people in charge of the Pref's persona. We realised that the strategy to establish a rapprochement with the city's public has been successful so far, and is also in line with the theoretical concepts discussed in this chapter that suggest the search for new forms of relationship between public or private institutions and their respective publics and/or consumers. So far, we have also been able to see the importance of creating a brand personality for companies that want to be on a social network. The creation of this persona contributes to the process of creating content that offers a greater chance of engagement with the public.

---

24 Available at: https://www.facebook.com/PrefsCuritiba/photos/a.516441535066322.1073741830.515514761825666/970356686341469/?type=3&theater Accessed on 28/04/2016)

In the next chapter we will show how the process of constructing a message for social networks takes place, as well as analysing other Pref's posts on social networks based on theoretical concepts of message creation and propagation. This study will allow us to assess how and in what context Pref's posts were devised.

CHAPTER 2

THE DEVELOPMENT OF THE MESSAGE: COMMUNICATION THEORIES THAT ARE PART OF THE DAILY LIFE OF PREFS

Messages are shared all the time on social networks around the world. Some of this content achieves significant numbers of views and interactions. In this chapter, we will look at theories that contribute to analysing the process of creating, interpreting and propagating digital messages through digital social networks, with a view to evaluating alternatives to understand what leads certain messages to reach a larger audience. Understanding this process will help us understand how Pref's creates its content and perhaps explain, at least in part, the success they have achieved with their Facebook page.

Constructing a message is an elaborate and complex activity. Channels such as blogs, social networks and digital portals are available to Internet users, offering a wide range of information that vies for the user's attention screen by screen. However, producing content that reaches a large number of people is still an arduous task for most professionals working in the field of digital marketing, since there is currently a very large volume of information circulating on the web (and users are free to follow these channels or not). In this way, the creation of content for digital channels can utilise theoretical concepts that support messages reaching a significant number of people.

One of the processes of message construction and the way in which it is transmitted and received was analysed in the article "Encoding / Decoding" written by Stuart Hall (2003)[25] , a Jamaican cultural theorist and sociologist who lived and worked in the UK from 1951. Hall, along with Richard Hoggart, EJ Thompson and Raymond Williams, was one of the central figures in what is now known as British Cultural Studies.

In that article, the author discusses the process of information circulation, classifying it as non-linear; in other words, there is not just the sender, the message and the receiver. Hall (2003) starts from the concept described by Marx (1982), who states that production determines consumption, just as consumption also determines production. Consequently, there is no deterministic view of reception (consumption) and production. "Production is therefore immediately consumption; consumption is immediately production. Each is immediately its opposite. But at the same time there is a mediating movement between the two" (MARX, 1982, p.08). Since there is no determinism in the production/consumption relationship, reception cannot be problematised in a homogenous way either. For Hall (2003), production in communication appears in the form of symbolic vehicles inserted into language rules. The circulation and consumption of this product takes place in discursive form. At the end, the discourse must be translated, and meaning may or may not be apprehended from it as previously planned. The stages of this process are presented as production, circulation, consumption/distribution and reproduction, but they are distinct and independent, in other words, one moment

---

[25] The study was carried out in the 1970s, but in this dissertation we have used the translation of the article published in 2003.

cannot guarantee the perfect existence of the next moment to which it is linked.

This model can be used to analyse messages posted on the Internet, especially on social networks. The messages that are published follow their own characteristics and generally come with a context that explains or translates that meaning, causing the content to be replicated. What we can see in this communication format is precisely the story behind the message (production). It can be seen that each message, when posted on a social networking channel (circulation), whether personal or corporate, is wrapped up in some context so that it can be better assimilated (consumption) by those who receive it who, after absorbing that content, share it on their own network, thus replicating that message (reproduction).

The process of encoding the message imposes certain limits within which decoding will operate; in this way, the correspondence between the two stages of the circulation process is constructed. Message composition, then

> It's not natural, but the product of articulation between two distinct moments. And coding cannot simply determine or guarantee which decoding codes will be used. Otherwise, communication would be a perfectly equivalent circuit and each message would be a 'perfectly transparent' instance of communication (HALL, 2003, p.399).

To explain these variations in interpretation, Hall created a hypothetical analysis for decoding processes, based on three concepts: (i) A dominant or preferential position, when the meaning of the message is decoded according to the references of its construction; (ii) A negotiated position, when the meaning of the message is negotiated with the particular conditions of the receivers; (iii) An oppositional position, when the receiver understands the dominant proposal of the message, but interprets it according to an alternative reference structure (2003, p. 399 - 401). We can therefore attribute the first concept of analysis (preferential dominant) as being the desired one, regardless of the types of message used on social networks.

So, for a message to be understood, the recipient needs to recognise the context in which it was created. To better explain this idea, we'll refer to a concept that talks about order, repertoire and structure (NETTO, 1996, p.122). For Abraham Moles apud Coelho Netto (1996, p.122), "the message is an ordered group of elements of perception extracted from a repertoire and brought together in a certain structure". For this article we will focus on the concept of repertoire. A repertoire is understood as "a kind of vocabulary, a stock of signs known and used by an individual" (NETTO, 1996, p.123). For the author, the creator of the message uses a certain repertoire. The decoder of the message will use their own repertoire, and only when the two repertoires have something in common will the flow of communication tend to enable understanding according to the expectations of the creator (encoder) of the message (1996, p. 124). A message will be meaningful or not (it will have more or fewer changes) depending on whether or not the repertoire of that message belongs to the receiver's repertoire.

The significance of a repertoire for those who possess it is a function of their conditions of existence, of a personal history. In addition to specific technical knowledge, repertoire means all the ethical, aesthetic, philosophical and political values and ideology of the individual, group or social class. The greater the receiver's repertoire, the less redundant the message and vice versa. A message is elaborated by the source with elements drawn from a certain repertoire, and will be decoded by a receiver who, in the process, will use elements drawn from another repertoire. For the flow of communication to be established, for the message to be meaningful to the decoder, there needs to be an intersection between the repertoires of the source (encoder) and the decoder. If both repertoires are absolutely identical, what reaches the decoder will not change their behaviour. In the case of tangent repertoires, the receiver will see the message as something intriguing, therefore something to be unravelled. However, we also realise that some of the messages made available on the networks show a connotative aspect, i.e. they don't always convey the message in a direct and objective way, so their content requires interpretation based on the contexts in which the message was constructed, and there is an analytical distinction between denotation and connotation.

> Denotation would be used as the aspects of a sign that seem to be considered, in any community and at any time, as its 'literal' meaning; and connotation corresponds to the meanings that are generated in association with the sign. (HALL, 2003, p. 393)

It is in the connotative sphere that ideological values operate most strongly, since in this sphere meanings are not fixed in a naturalised perception, they are more open and more susceptible to transformation; "the field is thus opened up for ideologies to alter meaning, the class struggle of language is born" (HALL, 2003, p. 394).

Based on this concept, we can perhaps understand why the profile of many of the messages transmitted by social networks are always subjective, enigmatic, indirect or somewhat ironic messages that are made available at all times and need the process of circulating information in order to have the possibility of being decoded appropriately (according to the interests of the encoder).

The discussion about how a message is constructed and interpreted can also be complemented by the question: what causes certain messages to spread, be commented on and replicated?

To discuss this topic we will use an article by a Dutch sociologist, Rudd Koopmans (2004) entitled Movements and the media: selection processes and evolutionary dynamics in the public sphere[26] . Before starting the discussion, it is worth contextualising how and why this article was written.

Koopmans is a professor of sociology at the Free University of Amsterdam and conducts research into social movements, citizenship, integration, European politics and evolutionary sociology[27] . Due to his specialisation, the article aims to discuss how interactions between social movements and political authorities move from direct physical confrontation between them in concrete locations to indirect ones, i.e. those carried out through communication vehicles such as print and television newspapers that provide discussions, mediated in the public sphere and mass media. To do this, he uses social movements that took place in Germany in the early 1990s, shortly after the fall of the Berlin Wall. Even though Koopmans' study is aimed at traditional

---

[26] Free translation of the original title "Movements and media: Selection processes and evolutionary dynamics in the public sphere".

[27] Available at https://www.wzb.eu/en/persons/ruud-koopmans viewed on 07/01/2016.

mass media, we will use it in this discussion because his theory has been used as a basis for creating content on digital social networks, such as the Curitiba City Council's institutional Facebook page. The information regarding the use of the concept by the Pref's was reported to the author in an interview with Borba (2016)

For Koopmans (2004), there are three mechanisms he calls "discursive opportunities" that affect the possibilities of spreading controversial messages. These are visibility (the extent to which a message is covered by the mass media), resonance (the extent to which others - allies, opponents, authorities etc. - react to a message) and legitimacy (the degree to which these reactions are favourable). The argument shows how the strategic repertoire of the German radical right evolved over the course of the 1990s as a result of the differentiated reactions through strategies found in the mass media. In this chapter, we will only analyse the three opportunities, since they have been applied in the Pref's digital communication process. This public body uses these concepts to formulate its content for interaction with the residents who follow it and has been recognised for its work, according to an interview with the author[28] . After discussing this topic, it will be possible to establish a relationship between the two theories (Hall and Koopmans) and Pref's communication process.

Let's start by talking about visibility. "Visibility is a necessary condition for a message to influence public discourse" (KOOPMANS, 2004, p. 374). In other words, it's the extent of coverage that the mass media devote to a given topic. It is possible to observe that communication through digital social networks is more agile than traditional media (radio, television and newspapers) can keep up with, perhaps because in traditional media the information or news has a set time to reach the public, while on the Internet it can be accessed at any time (according to the wishes of the user and the message encoder). What we are also observing is a phenomenon of the mass media appropriating information from content made available on the Internet that has been widely shared or, as Koopmans (2004) calls it, resonated.

Visibility is a necessary condition for the communicative impact of a discursive message; however, it is likely to remain ineffective if it does not succeed in provoking reactions from other actors in the public sphere. This is exactly where resonance comes in, which, for Koopmans (2004), are the reactions of other actors to an original message that is reproduced until it reaches new audiences. "The messages that resonate are the ones that travel the furthest" (KOOPMANS, 2004, p.374). The process of a message resonating is directly linked to the concept of legitimacy, which is "the degree to which, on average, third-party reactions in the public sphere support or reject an agent or its claims" (KOOPMANS, 2004, p. 375). What is highly legitimate does not achieve significant resonance because it is uncontroversial. What is accepted by everyone as legitimate ends up not being replicated as a message. On the other hand, what the author calls "highly illegitimate" becomes extremely resonant, in other words, it increases the reach of that message, such as the

[28] Interview granted via e-mail by the director of the Internet and Social Media department at Curitiba City Hall, Álvaro Borba, in which he explains how the department works and how it is positioned to produce content for the City Hall Facebook page. Interview granted on 28/03/2016.

cases of violence he addresses in Germany with evidence of neo-Nazi participation in the movements studied. Using the concept of repertoire described by Coelho Netto (1996), we can reinforce this idea:

> If the two repertoires are totally external to each other, the information is not transmitted to the receiver. On the other hand, if both repertoires are absolutely identical (...) what reaches the receiver will in no way alter their behaviour because it is necessarily something they already know (NETTO, 1996, p 124).

To better exemplify these concepts, we can use a case that occurred in Curitiba in 2014 (although not related to Pref's), when an argument between a customer who was dissatisfied with the poor service she received in a bar in the city and the owner of the bar took on unexpected proportions (resonance): the case became known in many states in Brazil. At the time, the customer used Facebook to complain about the service and products offered by the establishment (figure 9).

In response, the owner of the establishment offended her and even lamented that "the food didn't hurt" her (customer) (figure 10). Very quickly, the case spread across the web and, within a few hours, there were already comments from people in other cities, as well as several other establishments that took advantage of the opportunity with messages of support for the customer, as well as taking the opportunity to invite the dissatisfied customer to visit their establishment .[29]

Juliana Cavalcante em Phoenix American Mex
Seguir
20 de abril às 11:19 · Curitiba

Phoenix American Mex nunca mais!!!
Não é que sou chata.. mas chegar a um bar onde a entrada não é barata, ser informada pela hosttes que mesas só na área externa mas quem em 1h +- poderemos ir pra área interna já não é de animar mas tudo bem ... (pensei que a area extrena seria de frente pra br onde da pra ver o salão mas ao ir pra essa tal área externa e ver que é um "puxadinho" totalmente isolado do resto do bar...penso bom vou aproveitar pra comer ... já que gosto de comida mexicana...(o barè classificado como "comida mexicana") olho o cardápio poucas opções (o preço tb não é dos melhores)... mas tá to com fome... peço ... não trazem sal nem palitos pra fritas da minha amiga, não trazem nem guardanapo... solicitamos tudo ao garçom(e depois dividimos com a mesa a lado que tb não tinha e o garçom tinha sumido!) a cerveja aquela que desce redondo (que tb lá não é barata) quente, comida é boa mas a quantidade... passam 3 h e nós ainda no puxadinho...vcs acham q a banda mexicana caracterizada que passava pelas mesas do salão passou pelo puxadinho ? Não,... do puxadinho nem da pra ver o salão e mal dava pra ouvir a banda de rock que veio depois a hosttes sumiu e "nosso nome na lista de espera pro salão tb" eu me senti em um buteco pé sujo pagando o mesmo que as outras pessoas que desfrutaram de um ambiente totalmente diferente um bar lindo bem decorado com som, show...
a e pra finalizar banheiros interditados....kakaakakaae logico na saída a conta bem salgada.... devia ter ido ao zapata! #phoenixamericanmex nunca mais!!!
#phoenixamericanmex nunca mais!!!#phoenixamericanmex nunca mais!!!

Curtir · Comentar · Compartilhar

Figura 9 - Customer Complaint on Social Media
SOURCE: Gazeta do Povo On-Line
http://www.gazetadopovo.com.br/economia/redamacao-de-diente-sobre-bar-de-curitiba-viraliza-nas-redes-sociais-8fofdgego16nv8tc3gfo8rjgu Accessed on 18/06/2016

[29] Other bars in the city showed their support by sending messages to the customer like this one: "Sorry Juuuu! Come and we'll serve you better and for you to be happy the 1ª bottle of Skol is on us ;)" available at http://musardos.com.br accessed on 07/01/2016

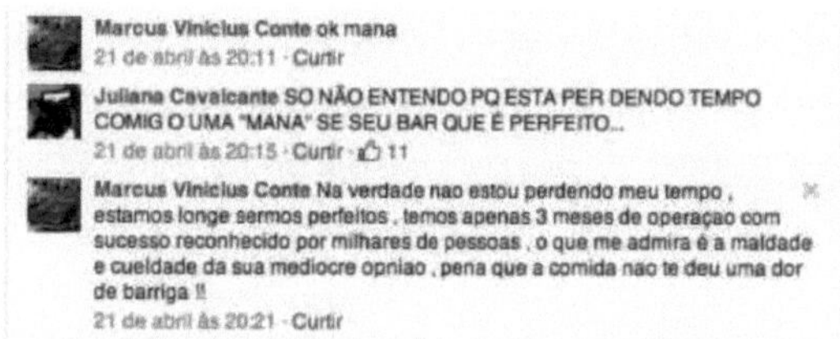

Figure 10 - Coarse response

SOURCE: Gazeta do Povo On-Line
http://www.gazetadopovo.com.br/economia/redamacao-de-diente-sobre-bar-de-curitiba-viraliza-nas-redes-sociais-8fofdgego16nv8tc3gfo8rjgu Accessed on 18/06/2016

We can therefore understand from Koopmans' study that a message will achieve resonance, i.e. it will be replicated through the available communication channels when there is a balance between what is highly legitimate, i.e. what is recognised as legitimate by users (such as the fact that the character featured in the text complains about the bar) and what is highly illegitimate (the bar owner's rude reaction).

> We can perhaps expect a curvilinear relationship between broadcast messages and their legitimacy, with messages whose legitimacy is controversial. They will generally be in a better position than any highly legitimate or highly illegitimate message. (KOOPMANS,2004, p. 375)

The concept can be represented by means of a graph (figure 11) which helps to better understand the meaning of this theory. We'll use the case of the complaint mentioned above to illustrate the points highlighted in the graph.

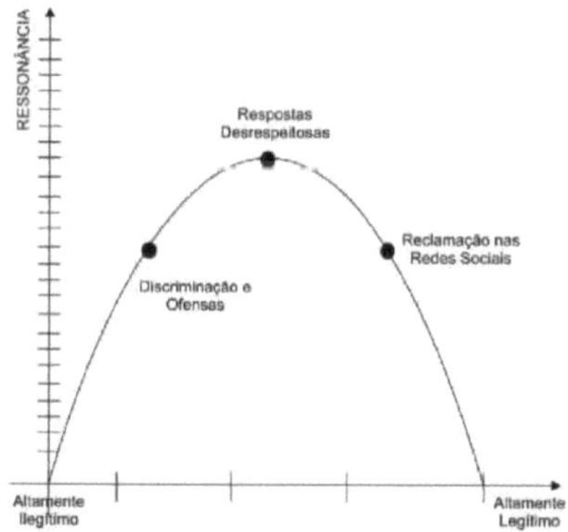

Figure 11 - Graph representing the concept of Resonance

Source: http://pt.slideshare.net/alvaroborba - Adapted by the author of this dissertation

Using the episode of the customer service complaint, we can apply the concepts described by Koopmans. The graph represents the scope of what happened, as the consumer's complaint (highly legitimate) is balanced against the offences and discrimination uttered by the bar owner (highly illegitimate). The balance between these two moments, which can be considered from the disrespectful responses, helped the episode to resonate, thus receiving a large number of shares on the web.

We can establish a relationship between Hall (2003) and Koopmans (2004) if we look at Pref's work. Creating a post involves a creative process, i.e. you have to plan, think and come up with concepts that can be better assimilated by the audience you want to reach. Hall (2003) argues that a message should be inserted into a circulation process, i.e. it needs to be translated into a context that allows the decoder to understand it,

Consequently, it must be replicated (shared when we talk about social networks). Koopmans (2004), in turn, understands that a message must create a certain balance between acceptance (highly legitimate) and denial (highly illegitimate). When this balance is reached, the message will then achieve resonance (again, a concept similar to sharing on social networks).

As we understand it, Pref's uses these two concepts (Koopmans certainly uses them, as the author of this dissertation was told in an interview) when creating its posts. The attempt to create a message that can be recognised and translated by its audience is part of the theoretical context described by Hall (2003). The use of symbols recognised by the internet users who follow Pref's on Facebook to talk about institutional matters (a topic that will be discussed in greater depth in chapter 3 of this research) struck a balance between the institutional and the stripped-down, through memes that use amusing language, but without losing the responsibility of dealing with matters relating to the City Hall, and in this way gave the messages resonance, making this content reach millions of people, many of them who did not live in (or are not from) the city of Curitiba. But it should be noted that the repertoire for decoding some of the messages is relatively limited, as discussed below.

A message that spreads and gains volume as it reaches more people is referred to in the context of the Internet as a viral message (MARTINO, 2014). In the digital environment, for something to become propagable, it needs to be on a network and, through it, reach a greater number of people. Talking to someone isn't necessarily a challenge for those who are present on Facebook. However, getting the public to interact with you becomes a challenge. As discussed in the previous chapter, in order for the communication process on a digital social network such as Facebook to achieve better results, i.e. to be able to reach a greater number of people, there needs to be interaction (likes, comments and shares) between the parties: this is organic reach .[30]

In this way, the concept of viralisation involves the individual and, consequently, their opinions, upbringing and beliefs. It is only when we reach these points for each individual that a message can be replicated. According to Martino (2014), using a study carried out by Shifman[31] , "in the case of virals, the

[30] Organic reach on Facebook refers to the number of people reached spontaneously without the use of advertising. This process is achieved as the followers of a profile (or page) interact with posts through likes, comments and shares. Available at: https://www.facebook.com/help/285625061456389 accessed on 21/08/2016.

[31] Quote from the book Social Media Theory in which the author presents a table to demonstrate factors that make a message viral, a table based on the article by Shifman L. **Memes in Digital Culture**. Presented at the MIT Press in 2014 (p. 180).

emotional charge is relevant to the extent that their sharing depends, in principle, on the impact caused" (2014, p. 180). Therefore, the propagation of a message through the network depends on the interpersonal relationship that the individual establishes, i.e. even though it passes through the individual sphere, messages gain the Network when there is a feeling that that content will be of interest to more people and, consequently, is shared in their own network. This concept is known as propagability:

> Spreadability refers to the technical resources that make it easier for some types of content to circulate compared to others, there are economic structures that support or restrict circulation, the attributes of a media text that can arouse a community's motivation to share material and the social networks that connect people through the exchange of meaningful bytes. (JENKINS; GREEN; FORD, 2014, p. 19)

According to the authors, "propagability recognises the importance of social connections between individuals" (p. 20). Thus, once again we realise the need to develop something that can reach the decoder's repertoire, since for a message to be shared, it needs to have a direct relationship with the context in which the person receiving that message lives. It is likely that if this is recognised, sharing will be more likely to happen. In addition to this, we can also emphasise the need to be part of a group and interact with it. Even if the message doesn't reach the decoder directly, it is often shared as a form of socialisation.

To better contextualise this subject, we will use Noelle Neumann's (1974, 1984, 1991) concept of the Spiral of Silence, described in Denis McQuail's book Theories of Mass Communication (2013). The concept was developed and tested by the researcher and addresses issues related to four elements: mass media, interpersonal communication and social relations, individual expressions of opinion and the individual's perceptions of the so-called climate of opinion. The premises of this concept are described as follows by McQuail (2013, p.489): (i) Society threatens deviant individuals with isolation; (ii) These individuals are continually afraid of isolation; (iii) This fear of isolation causes individuals to try to assess the climate of opinion at all times; (iv) The results of this assessment affect their behaviour in public, especially their willingness or unwillingness to express opinions openly.

Generally speaking, the theory is based on the idea that people make decisions based on what they believe to be "majority decisions" (MCQUAIL, 2013p. 489). Even though the study was designed to assess the prevailing climate in mass media, we can relate the result to what happens on social networks. On these channels, content achieves views when it reaches individuals who are interconnected through common interests. However, when these individuals represent a large number, the message gains traction with other people who may not have the same interests, but end up realising that the content is being seen by many users on the network. This would be the fear of isolation (cited by Neumann in his study) that affects Internet users all over the world, causing messages to be shared on the Internet simply because the content is propagated by a large number of people.

Pref's uses the theory proposed by Koopmans (2004) as a basis[32]. According to this author's study, if there is consensus, there is no dialogue:

> it's clear that a town hall has little to say that isn't a consensus. We can't take away the legitimacy of our institutional messages. So we combine educational, citizenship or service messages, which are legitimate and consensual, with a non-consensual aesthetic. (BORBA, 2016)

Although this statement brings us back to what could be a kind of Agenda Setting (MCCOMBS; SHAW, 1972), we believe that the context studied is more related to the concept of Agenda-melding, which is

> the way in which we balance civil community agendas and our community reference values to create a satisfactory picture of the world. Agenda-melding does not replace agenda-setting, but seeks to explain why the strength of media agenda-setting varies between different media, groups and individuals (SHAW; WEAVER, 2014, p. 145).

According to Koopmans' theory (2004), it takes boldness, taking people out of their comfort zone, by means of provocative and even controversial messages, for a piece of content to be able to be discussed and achieve the propagability mentioned by Jenkins, Green and Ford (2014). A good example of this is the case in which Curitiba City Hall, through its communications department, created a fake campaign in 2015 (figure 12), with the aim of provoking people with a controversial topic: the rights of disabled people. The campaign initially advocated an end to the rights of disabled people, which immediately caused a lot of buzz[33], including from vehicles considered to be mass media. Even with a lot of criticism, the campaign reached a large number of people so that the real message it was intended to spread (which was in favour of disability rights) was then propagated (figure 13).

Figure 12 OutDoor of the fake campaign advocating an end to disabled people's rights. Source: Google Images

---

[32]As mentioned in an interview with the author of this research, Alvaro Borba (2016) claims to have Koopmans' theory as his theoretical basis. The interview can be found in ANNEX II of this dissertation

[33] A term meaning "noise" that is generally used in marketing actions to attribute content that has a good impact.

Figure 13 Image published on social networks with the true content of the campaign Source: Google Images

In fact, there is no recipe to follow. Cross-referencing information, theories and concepts can help communication professionals use the best strategies to reach their audience, whether that audience is made up of friends who are part of a small network, a city, a country or the whole world .

2.1 - MESSAGES AND MEMES

Writing a text, taking a photo or recording a video are common actions nowadays due to the technological apparatus available. The tools we have at our disposal allow us to record and tell stories all the time, most of the time about ourselves. According to Sibilia (2008):

> millions of users all over the planet - "ordinary" people just like you and me - have taken advantage of the various online tools that are constantly emerging and expanding, and used them to publicly expose their intimacy. This has created a veritable festival of 'private lives'. (p.26)

The author's discourse is quite synergistic with the times we live in. The lives of many people who use digital social networks, in particular, are no longer just their own property, they are shared with the Net. This exposure has brought with it an excessive need to make their lives an event. There is a competition, albeit unconscious, to see which posts get the most followers, the most likes and the most comments. What's interesting to note is that as technology advances, providing more capacity and technical quality in the production of content, the complexity of what is displayed also increases. We have at our disposal a series of small directors, copywriters and designers who create content in video, text and images. And it is precisely these images, known as memes, that are gaining more and more space on digital networks.

> an 'idea meme' can be defined as an entity capable of being transmitted from one brain to another. The meme of Darwin's theory, therefore, is the essential foundation of the idea that is shared by all the brains that understand it, (DAWKINS, 2007, p. 217-218).

The basic characteristics of this phenomenon, according to this study, are: "longevity" (if it is legitimate, i.e. recognised by several people, it needs to last); "fidelity" (once legitimate, it remains faithful to the idea that originated it) and "fecundity" (a legitimate meme is widely replicated to evolve in different ways).

Based on Dawkins' study, which presents the meme as the gene of culture, Recuero (2007) developed a study on the application of this form of communication in weblogs, thus proposing a classification of these icons, dividing them according to the following criteria: fidelity of the copy, longevity, fecundity and reach.

Copy fidelity refers to the meme's similarity to its original. The greater the retention of its original characteristics, the greater the fidelity of the copy. On this criterion, they are divided into replicators and mimetics defined as follows:

(i) **Replicators (figure 14)**: are those whose basic characteristic is reduced variation, with high fidelity to the original copy.

(ii) **Mimetics (figure 15)**: these are memes that, despite undergoing mutations and recombinations, maintain the same structure, which is why they are referred to as imitations. They can be adapted to the characteristics of the channel in which they will be used.

Figure 14 - Example of a replicating meme: Obama "Not bad"

Figure 15 Example of a mimetic meme: Keep Calm

Longevity, on the other hand, refers to the meme's existence over time, i.e. the longer it survives, the greater its chance of replicating itself. However, on the Internet it can be archived and reappear after a while. Thus, in this category they are defined as persistent and volatile:

(i) **Persistent (figure 16):** those that remain reproduced for a long time, i.e. they are not restricted to a particular moment.

(ii) **Volatile (figure 17): these** are those that have a short life span, i.e. they are reproduced on one or other blog (or social network), but are later forgotten or modified; in the latter case, a new meme is created.

Figura 16 - Exemplo de meme persistente: Rage Comics

Figura 17 - Exemplo de meme volátil: "Luiza está no Canadá"

Figure 16 - Example of a persistent meme: Rage Comics
Figure 17 - Example of a volatile meme: "Luiza is in Canada"

The concept of fecundity refers to the number of replications of a meme and its speed. Since memes are archived on the Internet, fecundity is seen as their ability to spread. In this category they are divided into epidemic and fecund: (i) **Epidemic (figure 18):** epidemic memes are those with high fecundity, which spread widely through social networks, like an epidemic.

(iii) **Fecund (figure 19):** memes that don't become epidemic, but are spread by small groups on certain channels. It's worth noting that all memes are potentially fertile, even if there are different degrees of fertility.

Figura 18 - Exemplo de meme fecundo: T Rex Fanho

Figura 19 - Exemplo de meme epidêmico: Conselhos da Gina Indelicada

Figure 18 - Example of a fertile meme: T Rex Fanho
Figure 19 - Example of an epidemic meme: Advice from Impolite Gina

Finally, the author conceptualises reach as referring to which types of nodes[34] the meme reaches the most. Thus, memes in this category are divided into global and local:

(i) **Global (figure 20):** these are the ones that reach internet users and are far apart within a given social

[34] This concept of "nodes" in social networks has already been worked on earlier in this dissertation. See Chapter 01, page 09

network, i.e. they appear at points that are not close together .[35]

H) **WCaS^figure 21): These** are restricted to a particular weblog network. The sites are reproduced by people who are close to each other and have a higher level of interaction.

Figura 21 - Exemplo de meme local: Suricate Seboso

Figura 20 - Exemplo de meme global: Troll face

Figure 20 - Example of a global meme: Troll face
Figure 21 - Example of a local meme: Suricate Seboso

We can see that there are many possible formats for using memes in digital communication. It seems that even though they involve a creative process, aesthetic issues don't seem to concern users of this message format, since amateur productions are given the same space as creations made by professionals. It's worth having a brief discussion about the concept of aesthetics so that we can better understand how memes become a cultural manifestation of the Internet.

The communication process, especially advertising, has always prioritised the transmission of an impactful message, usually full of graphic quality and produced by qualified professionals. With the popularisation of the Internet and, above all, technology, we have realised that the preparation of these materials for communication in digital environments does not require the published materials to be "great masterpieces". It even seems that in many cases the opposite is true. The simpler (more amateurish) the creation is, the more propagation and dissemination effect it can have. We attribute this to the fact that less produced memes can be used several times, in various contexts, while a more elaborate creation tends to be used only for that specific purpose.

Part of this can be attributed to the technological ease of the digital world. Today we have several devices that are highly prepared for multifunctional applications, including image editing, photo and video capture and thousands of other applications that are launched daily. Even with all this technology at our

[35] We use the Trollface meme as an example for this category. This meme has various definitions, but generally refers to a "prick" who just wants to cause trouble. This characteristic is recognised by Internet users all over the world. Available at: http://www.tecmundo.com.br/memes/77923-trollface-nascimento-meme-deu-boa-grana-criador-problem.htm Accessed on: 15/08/2016

disposal, we realise that the quality of what is created can still be questioned when it comes to artistic production. Bosi (2002) addresses this issue when he says: "any human activity, as long as it regularly leads to an end, can be called artistic". (p.13). From this perspective, we can say that a meme is also a form of art. Now: is there really an aesthetic experience in this communication process using memes?

To do this, we turned to Gumbrecht's (2006) conceptualisation of the aesthetic experience:

> the aesthetic experience consists of the gradual process of emergence, rather than the imposed interruption or epiphany. To use the language of the Russian formalists: it is not the effect of a 'deautomatisation', but precisely the 'automatisation' of sitting comfort that can trigger our interest in its motives, thus transforming comfort into an aesthetic experience. (p.57)

With this in mind, we can reflect that the use of memes in digital communication can be considered an aesthetic experience, since it gives those who use social networks comfort in understanding the message. The extensive use of images, together with text, translates emotions that bring users closer together to the point where the message is shared thousands (even millions) of times across the networks. The process of constructing these messages seems to follow the model of a story, so that it can "go viral".

In this way, the process of constructing the message, using overlapping images and texts, encodes a message in an attempt to decode it clearly and objectively so that it can then be shared. Martino (2014) describes how the simplicity of the message contributes to its distribution on the web:

> the simplicity of the message, humour and the possibility of the public taking action to share the message are among the main ones. In the case of virals, the emotional charge is relevant to the extent that their sharing depends, in principle, on the impact caused. (p.180)

If Martino's (2014) statement is true, the aesthetic quality of the message has no impact on the result it aims to achieve. It is enough for the message to create an identity with a group, or a moment in anyone's life (repertoire) for it to become enjoyable, regardless of its aesthetic concept. Kant (2008), in his work Critique of the Faculty of Judgement, contributes to this reflection when he addresses issues related to the conceptualisation of what is beautiful and sublime. The philosopher reflects on natural beauty and is concerned with determining under what conditions it is possible for the judgement of taste to perceive beauty in things.

> The judgement of pleasantness refers to sociability, insofar as it is based on empirical rules. And although judgements concerning the good also rightly aspire to be valid for everyone, the good is represented only by means of a concept as the object of a general pleasure, which is not the case with the pleasant or the beautiful (KANT, 2008, p.56).

We agree with Kant to the extent that the question of whether a digital message is considered pleasant (tolerated) is related to its sociability (general pleasure), since what is accepted by the majority becomes an aesthetic concept for a certain segment (good, if we use what was described by Kant). A message will gain its place on the Net when it is recognised by a large number of people (users) who categorise it as good (pleasurable in Kant's view). In these cases, we see that this type of message ends up being shared repeatedly simply because a large number of people are taking the initiative and not necessarily because they liked the message. To explain this idea better, we refer again to Noelle Neumann's concept (1974, 1984, 1991) which is based on the concept that people make decisions based on what they believe to be "majority decisions" (p. 489). We realise that although there is an individual aesthetic concept (taste according to Kant's analysis), the use of memes in digital communication does not appropriate concepts linked to individual taste, but rather what is recognised by the masses in the language of the medium in which it is used (the Internet). In this way, we consider that the whole aesthetic process of a digital message is based on the cultural group identity it provides to those who use this communication mechanism. In other words, each group will use its own aesthetic experiences to communicate, and the message that fulfils its role of cultural identity will be recognised as beautiful or pleasant.

Certain behaviours that we observe in different social groups can be recognised as cultural actions of that universe of people. In this way, we can see that the use of the Internet, anywhere in the world, provides behaviours that create group identity, recognition that, in order to use this or that network, their behaviour has to be in line with mass behaviour.

If we can define this type of behaviour as mass behaviour, then we can also call it cultural behaviour. Williams (1969) defines culture as follows: "Culture used to mean a state or habit of mind, or a body of intellectual and moral activities; now it means a whole way of life" (p.20). The way of life on social networks is only valued when it uses tools that are recognised by the users of that channel. Memes have this identity function to the extent that they become the tool that allows people to recognise something as being "from the Internet".

Memes are transmitted between people and, due to the speed with which they spread, they become cultural tools that go beyond interpersonal relationships (MARTINO, 2014). "This relationship between the micro level of individual sharing and the macro level of social reach makes memes particularly important for understanding contemporary culture" (p. 178). Martino, using Limor Shifman's (2014) article[36] as a reference, cites the author's classification of "all digital culture, with its copies, transformations and sharing of information, as being part of a hypermimetic process" (p.178). It is precisely the fact that memes are tools for spreading messages that makes them mechanisms for cultural recognition of those who use the Internet. It seems that society is converging towards a new way of communicating:

> Convergence doesn't happen through devices, however sophisticated they may be. Convergence takes place inside the brains of individual consumers and in their social interactions with others. Each of us builds our own personal mythology, from bits and pieces of information extracted from the media flow and transformed into resources through which we understand our daily lives. (JENKINS, 2006, pg.30)

But why do memes work? To possibly explain this, Martino (2014) uses two concepts described by

[36] The article by Shifman L. **Memes in Digital Culture** was presented at the MIT Press in 2014 (p. 180) and is referenced in Martino's (2014) book discussing the use of memes on the internet.

Shifman. The first is the economic issue, in which, according to the author, in times of an information economy, "getting people's attention is a valuable commodity" (p.179). The second point is related to the creation of bonds, however superficial, between people:

> To rework a meme is to be part of a community that may be anonymous, but is no less strong. Memes are shared on digital social networks, in a way, for the same reason that people tell jokes or stories they've heard: to be part of the group. (MARTINO, 2014 p.179)

In this way, the creation of memes provides a narrative that aims to establish links between people who use digital channels. These messages tend to be decoded appropriately by people who use that group, who have the same repertoire. When you understand a meme, it means that you are part of that group and that you can decode messages that are not always clear to those who are not part of that context, i.e. who do not have the same cultural identity.

In Pref's case, the use of memes ended up becoming the most common way of communicating via its Facebook page. The use of this type of post enabled the institution to get closer to an audience that until then had not interacted (at least not often) with Curitiba City Hall. Some of the most prominent posts used elements in which the issue of identity through repertoire is evident and is perceived (decoded) by the public in a more intuitive way. It is worth emphasising that it was not possible to establish a pattern with regard to the concepts of what is viral (MARTINO, 2014) or propagable (JENKINS, GREEN, FORD 2014) in the posts published by the Pref's, since we observed both situations being applied.

Below we will list some of these posts, showing how the concepts and theories discussed in this chapter were used in the process of constructing institutional messages. It is worth noting that all the posts we will list always use a pop culture repertoire to convey an institutional message.

The first post we've highlighted is a message aimed at informing residents about renovations to the city's bus terminals that would make one of the city's most used bus routes, the "Inter 2", more agile. To catch the public's attention, the Pref's team used a reference from the American series Game of Thrones, originally produced by the pay-TV channel HBO, the first chapter of which is entitled "Winter is Coming". The expression has become common jargon among fans of the series. Taking advantage of this moment, Pref's made a post (Figure 22) on taking advantage of the similar sound of the word Winter with Inter[37] , thus creating the expression "Inter is coming!". It's important to emphasise that the idea came from a Pref's follower, duly referenced in the post, thus showing the synergy between the institution and its public.

---

[37] In the city of Curitiba, one of the bus routes that runs between the city's neighbourhoods is called Interbairros. Each neighbourhood has an Interbairros line identified by numbers, e.g. Interbairros 1, 2, 3, etc. One of these lines, which uses a different system, the so-called ligeirinhos, is called Inter 2 and is one of the most used in the city, as its route is one of the longest.

Figure 22 - Inter is Coming!
Source: Curitiba City Hall Fanpage.

The second post we're going to list uses the success of a cartoon series called "Adventure Time[38] ". In this series, the main character Finn and his dog Jake experience various unusual situations in the Land of Ooo. The series was particularly popular with young audiences in 2013 and 2014. It also attracted the attention of adults because the cartoon made references that could be understood by a more mature audience[39] . Because of this recognition, Pref's used its characters to convey a storm warning message. In the post (figure 23) we see the two main characters travelling on the back of another, Lady Iris (who is half unicorn, half rainbow). The post also uses irony to inform us that the image is not real, as it is impossible to "surf on a rainbow" on a cloudy day. Along with the joke comes a warning for people to avoid heavy clouds.

Figure 23 - Adventure Time
Source: Curitiba City Hall Fanpage

Another post we've picked out uses a reference that has become well known on the web due to an advert on a website for buying and selling products. In the commercial, the artist Cumpadi Washington, who rose to fame with the

[38] Cartoon series that tells the adventures of the boy Finn and his dog Jake. Available at http://www.cartoonnetwork.com.br/show/hora-de-aventura accessed on 25/05/2016.

[39] The cartoon was so successful that it was given a film version, according to an article available at http://otvfoco.com.br/desenho-de-maior-sucesso-atualmente-hora-de-aventura-ira-para-as-telonas/ accessed on 25/05/2016

pagode group "É o Tchan", appears as if he were a radio that annoys the residents of a house (especially the owner of the house) with heavy and, to a certain extent, offensive expressions. At one point he asks: "Is this your husband? You know nothing, innocent![40] ". This expression (which was also used by the musician in several of the group's songs) quickly made its way around the web via various memes that used the expression as a way of denying something. Pref's then decided to publish a newspaper report (figure 24) that told how to visualise a total lunar eclipse that would take place on that date. Making fun of the fact that the city of Curitiba's sky is often covered by clouds, they made a post in which, supposedly, the clouds themselves used the expression "you know nothing innocent", referring to the impossibility of following the natural phenomenon in the city.

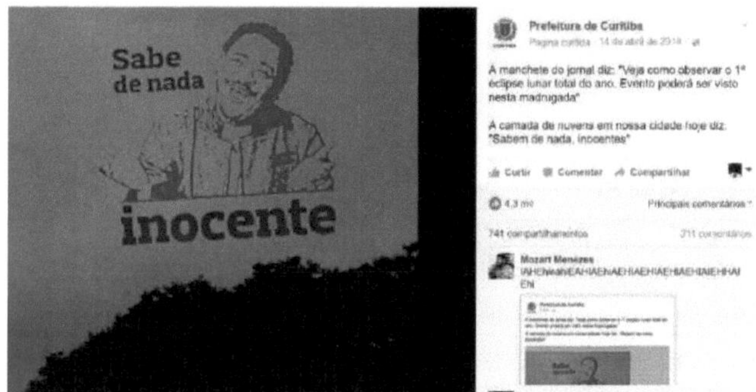

Figure 24 - You know nothing, Innocent!
'Source: Curitiba City Hall Fanpage.

The last post we've picked out here to comment on was published on Twitter, and took advantage of the characters in the Harry Potter film sequel. In these films, the main characters are young wizards who go on adventures at a school where they learn witchcraft. In the story, all those who aren't wizards are called "Wizards" by the characters. Using the image of the little wizards in a car, Pref's made a reference to the fact that young people shouldn't turn the city into a "troupe" by riding in the bus-only lane (called a canaleta by the city's residents). In the post (figure 25), a montage of young people in a car was placed in front of a city bus with a message warning about the exclusive use of these roads by buses.

[40] The expression had already been used in the group's songs, but it gained repercussions when it was mentioned in the commercial. The commercial can be watched at the following link: https://www.youtube.com/watch?v=d3dreI6mk g accessed on: 25/05/2016

Figure 25 - Harry Potter in the car.
Source: Curitiba City Hall Twitter account

Looking at these messages, we can once again see the great importance of the decoder's repertoire in the process of understanding the message. It seems clear that in order for the message to reach a greater number of people, recognising the context in which it was constructed can make a difference to the result the message will achieve. Pref's used this and various other contexts to make the public that uses social networks and has an interest in pop culture accept it and refer to it as one of the leading cases in terms of content management and digital relationships[41] . In fact, since the posting of the dementors (figure 5), it can be inferred that Pref's team found it possible to code most of their messages with this type of repertoire in mind. In the next chapter of this research, we'll delve deeper into the subject of relationships, trying to better understand how getting closer to its audience can lead to better results in terms of the City Council's interaction with the city's citizens.

[41] Media outlets across the country have reported on Pref's work, as can be seen in the article in the newspaper O Globo highlighting its work with good humour, but also with social actions. Available at: http://oglobo.globo.com/brasil/Prefeitura-de-curitiba-faz-sucesso-nas-redes-com-pagma- que-equilibra-humor-prestacao-de-servico-16490387 accessed on 05/06/2016

CHAPTER 3

MORE THAN A POST: USING RELATIONSHIPS AS A FORM OF DIGITAL COMMUNICATION

An institution's presence on the Internet is realised through various relationship channels. We'll cover this topic in the course of this chapter, using the concept of Relationship Marketing.

This type of marketing is used by companies all over the world as a way of building customer loyalty and investing less capital in acquiring new customers. With Pref's, the concept is gaining strength through the use of digital channels aimed at establishing closer contact with its residents. Even though this institution doesn't sell any specific product, using the relationship strategy favours institutional messages reaching a greater number of people, who are supposed to be informed about the city's events and also about the work of their town hall. The main aim of this chapter is to analyse Pref's actions through its posts, which, much more than building relationships and gaining a large audience, also transmit institutional messages that, through the relationship they have built and maintained, reach a significant number of people.

Being present on the Internet (mainly through social networks) opens up the possibility for institutions to interact with the people who are part of their network. Before the technological devices we have at our disposal today, contact between an institution and its public was made through physical presence, telephone or correspondence. It was usually one-sided, meaning that when someone needed something from that company, they would go to it to fulfil that specific need and then the relationship between the two parties could go on for long periods without any interaction. If the initiative didn't come from the consumer, it was the company that, through advertising, most of the time "sought out" its customers in order to draw the attention of its target audience to offers, news and other manifestations.

In these models, we realise that if it wasn't for a commercial reason, i.e. the purchase of a product, it is very unlikely that a relationship would be built between a company and its public. Contact between companies and customers only took place when the purchasing process was in evidence. Good customer service meant leading your customer to a good purchase; after that, there was a distancing between the parties until a new purchase was necessary. As the years went by, and competition increased, it became effective to compete for customers only with the best price and not with the best price.
always results in good results, Relationship Marketing has emerged in an attempt to change this process.

3.1 - RELATIONSHIP MARKETING

In response to the new reality of closer ties between customers and companies, the 1990s saw the emergence of a new marketing approach called "relationship marketing" (MACKENNA, 1993), when consumers became more demanding, wanting clear, precise, fast and real-time answers, as well as wanting to be treated differently, i.e. wanting special attention to be paid to their needs. This new way of marketing has made it possible for relationships between organisations and customers to become more lasting than simple one-off transactions.

The definition of a relationship[42] that we used earlier shows that in order to build a relationship it is necessary to establish social or emotional links with others. This concept seems to be common in relationships between people or between companies/institutions and people. We are therefore going to use Peppers and Rogers' (2004) definition to explain the importance of relationship marketing in institutions.

The authors build this concept based on a process for the relationship to consolidate. To start this relationship process, there needs to be a learning period in which the company learns about an individual customer through its transactions and interactions during the process of doing business. The customer, in turn, learns about the company through their successive purchasing experiences and other interactions. Realising this, the authors point out that a relationship is made up of the following concepts: reciprocity, interaction, exclusivity and trust (PEPPERS; ROGERS, 2004, p. 35-39). We're going to focus on the first two concepts because we believe that they are an integral part of Pref's communication process with its public, without discarding the others, as they are also part of a relationship process.

The first part of this process implies that every relationship needs reciprocity. To be considered a relationship, both parties have to participate and be aware of the existence of the relationship. This means that relationships must be two-way. In other words, the two parties involved must recognise that there is a relationship between them. According to the concept worked out by the authors, you can't have a relationship with another person if they don't have a relationship with you.

Bringing this concept into the corporate environment, can a person have a genuine relationship with a brand? Peppers and Rogers (2004) say yes, but this doesn't just happen because the customer likes the brand and buys its products repeatedly. A customer can have great affection for a brand alone, but a relationship between the customer and the brand can only exist if the brand (i.e. the company behind the brand) is also aware that the customer exists (creating demonstrations of this awareness), thus providing a two-way street and individualising the entire service process.

This vision becomes clear in Pref's actions if we look at the moment when the persona was constituted. In the episode in which a user commented on dementors in a post published by Pref's, and then the institution produced a patronum post to combat the dementors, at that moment reciprocity was established between the parties and the user wasn't just another one: they became unique.

The second important point to emphasise is that relationships are driven by interaction. When two parties interact, they exchange information and this exchange of information is a central driver for building the relationship. This, of course, also implies reciprocity. But interactions don't have to take place in a specific place, such as on the phone, in a personal service or on the Internet. Interaction occurs when a customer buys a product from the company, or in Pref's case, interacts with the post by commenting, liking or sharing the

[42] Already used in this dissertation in chapter 01, p 10.

message. Each interaction contributes to the total amount of information possible in the relationship. We can say that, in the case of work on social networks, achieving an interaction corresponds to achieving a product sale, since these channels aim to establish contact with their audience through messages that are intended to reach a significant number of people; thus, establishing an interaction can be considered a goal achieved.

For these reasons, organisations in general are also trying to get to know consumers better, listening to them, dedicating themselves to them, pleasing them and anticipating their wishes; in short, captivating them in such a way as to align the company with customers who value what it has to offer (IAN, 1999, p.106). In this new form of commercial relationship, also known as one-to-one marketing, a concept based on the paradigm that the future will be increasingly characterised by individualised relationships, business (commercial relationships) will be made up of increasingly personalised production and individual marketing made up of increasingly specific media, it can be seen that the business landscape is being radically transformed. Peppers and Rogers (1994) coined the term and believed that, in the future, the marketing process would be directed at one customer at a time. In this scenario, businesses will focus less and less on immediate profits from short- and medium-term sales figures, and their main objective will be to realise long-term profits by retaining customers for the long term and starting to develop lifelong relationships with them. "In the one-to-one future, it won't be how much you know about all your customers, but how much you know about each of your customers." (PEPPERS; ROGERS, 1994, p.7)

The Internet has taken on a strong role as the most cost-effective source of information, as it is visual, audible, interactive and in real time, as well as significantly altering organisations' relationships with customers, suppliers and consumers. The changes are considered to be a fundamental remodelling of the sector (WEBSTER, 1992) and are directed towards relationship marketing, the concept of which encompasses relational marketing, working partnerships, symbiotic marketing, relational retailing and internal marketing. Relationship marketing is therefore part of a developing network paradigm, which recognises that global competition is increasingly taking place between networks of organisations. The result of these global dynamics in the paradoxical nature of relationship marketing is that in order to be an effective competitor in a global economy, it is necessary to be a reliable co-operator in some part of the network.

> Experience-based marketing emphasises interactivity, connectivity and creativity. With this approach, companies dedicate themselves to their customers, constantly monitor their competitors and develop a feedback analysis system that transforms this information about the market and the competition into new and important information about the product. (MCKENNA, 1993 p. 47)

In the digital environment, social networks generally take on this role of centralising tool, since they bring together clients and companies, users and institutions, in Pref's case. There are a number of advantages to using these channels to build a closer relationship with your audience.

One of the main advantages of being present on a social network is the possibility of discovering customer needs. Pages created on platforms such as Facebook give consumers the opportunity to reveal their real needs, which gives the company a greater understanding of consumer desires and a better chance of catering for the target audience. Through relationship marketing, new ideas can emerge for the business and improvement will be continuous. Customers themselves are able to contribute to increasing the quality of the product offered, through suggestions, requests and information about what works well and what needs to be improved. A company that manages to see customers as strong allies for business growth tends to grow more and more and stand out in the market. Kevin Roberts (2004) uses the Lovemark concept, which advocates full knowledge (on the part of the company) of its audience. It involves getting to know your audience in an individualised way, knowing what they like and, above all, what they expect from your brand. For Roberts (2004), the relationship between consumer and brand is like a courtship and needs to follow the path of love: creating lasting and loyal emotional connections throughout life. Jenkins (2008) approaches the subject through the concept of affective economics, which according to him is "understanding the emotional underpinnings of consumer decision-making as a driving force behind audience and purchasing decisions" (2008, p. 96). Thus, the concepts of affective economy (JENKINS, 2008) and Lovemakers (ROBERTS, 2004) are connected since both depend directly on audience participation, either to understand their emotional foundations or to provide ways for consumers to express their "passion", engagement and opinions.

Another important factor is to assess the level of customer satisfaction, since dissatisfaction should be seen as an opportunity to improve the company's processes. If we think of a page on any social network as an extension of a company's brand, we realise that this brand is always being evaluated by the public and the concept can easily rise or fall. Regardless of the company's objectives, behaving in a way that prioritises social equality, fraternity, environmental preservation and solidarity can be very positive for a company's image. As a public institution, we've seen these concepts worked on frequently by Pref's in its posts.

Interacting with customers is much more than answering suggestions, complaints and solving problems involving sales. Through interaction, you can increase your audience and keep your followers up to date with all the latest news. It's important that your pages are always updated with interesting content that provokes interaction.

As far as Pref's work is concerned, we can say that the basis for the development of the work carried out by the team in charge of the official channels is to seek a relationship with its citizens. The department's main objective is to win media space rather than buy it. For this to be possible, it is necessary to rely on the viralisation potential of messages on the web (BORBA, 2016). In this way, investing in relationships and, above all, producing content that provides this relationship, is fundamental for these messages to be identified and recognised by those who receive them .[43]

For Ian (1999), relationships are the only really important asset, because they can bring long-term results. Through this learning relationship, it is possible to create bonds with your audience. Bogmann (2000)

---

[43] See the concept of repertoire described in chapter 2, p. 31 of this research (NETTO, 1996).

comments that relationship marketing has five levels to overcome with customers: a) basic - the product is sold, but there is no after-sales service; b) reactive - the sale is made and customers are encouraged to return if they have any doubts or possible problems; c) reliable - there is an after-sales service. The customer's opinion on the sale is sought; d) proactive - the sale is followed up with periodic calls to the customer to improve or offer new products; e) partnership - the company focuses on the customer to identify ways of offering better value. Reflecting on these concepts and seeking to make a direct relationship with the object of study of this research, we realise that in the channels in which Pref's operates, the partnership level is the most evident, since it is necessary for users, in general, to replicate its content so that the message reaches a greater number of people.

Complementing the universe of relationships, we can consider four points that are fundamental to establishing closer contact between an institution and its target audience. These points have been named the 4Rs (NETO, On-line) and are organised as follows: (i) Recognition - which is divided into establishing a corporate identity, brand management, brand image and institutional advertising. (ii) Relationships - which, within the scope of public relations, is a specific subject that requires specialised management. It can be divided into: internal public relations, external public service, ombudsman and conflict mediation. (iii) Relevance - in which it is necessary to understand which characteristics make us more relevant in the face of the immense quantity of the same services, products, among others. It can be divided into: opinion research, sponsorship, events and social marketing. (iv) Reputation - building a reputation is something that will come from a succession of attitudes, decisions, communications with the public and support for third-party projects; it also adds that: coherence, attachment to consolidated principles and values contribute to building a good reputation.

The importance of establishing a relationship between a legal person and an individual seems obvious. It is part of a strategic context used by companies all over the world. Maintaining constant contact with clients, or in the case of our object of study in this research, users who stay connected to an institution via a social network, has proved to be a complex task, mainly due to the large amount of information available on the Internet. Using Facebook alone, we can see that a user of this network can connect with several other institutions of interest. When using this digital social network, all you have to do is like a particular page for the content posted on it to reach the user who liked it. This means that a single user can receive posts from several institutional pages, i.e. from the pages of companies or legal entities.

With the growth in the use of Facebook by companies, the social network itself has started to restrict the reach[44] that these pages have so that the relationship between (natural) people is favoured. Thus, for a company to reach more people, its posts need to garner a large number of interactions with its followers; in this way, Facebook's algorithm understands that if a person is interacting with that page, it is because they are

[44] This information can also be analysed in the questions and answers section of the social network itself at: https://www.facebook.com/business/news/BR-Alcance-organico-no-Facebook- your-questions-answered Accessed on: 18/06/2016

interested in the content it publishes; consequently, the Fanpage's posts will appear more frequently for the interested user. Therefore, the relationship becomes a fundamental part of the communication process through channels like Facebook.

3.2 - PREF'S AND RELATIONSHIPS

The mission of keeping users interested in the content posted on Facebook seems even more difficult if we analyse the concept of Liquid Love described by Bauman (2004). The author writes about the fragility of relationships, a concept from which we can develop interesting reflections for this research. Our society has shown itself to be consumerist, in which relationships are based on interest and the "law of least effort" prevails:

> and so it is in a consumerist culture like ours, which favours the product ready for immediate use, fleeting pleasure, instant satisfaction, results that don't require prolonged effort, tested recipes, full insurance guarantees and money back. The promise of learning the art of love is the offer (false, misleading, but one fervently wishes it were true) to construct the 'love experience' like other commodities, which fascinate and seduce by displaying all these characteristics and promise desire without anxiety, effort without sweat and results without effort. (BAUMAN, 2004, p.11)

It was precisely realising the fragility of relationships as described by Bauman (2004) that gave rise to an interest in understanding how actions promoted by Pref's materialise beyond published posts using the power of relationships on a digital social network.

The ease of finding information on the Internet would make relationships even more superficial, since the information that matters could be on several channels. Maintaining loyalty to a particular channel will depend on what kind of effort that channel will make to keep the user's attention, as the user will be able to move around the web in search of what suits them best, without having to wait.

It seems that this characteristic is present in our current relationships. For a relationship to last, you need to invest; in other words, you need to constantly maintain the relationship with your partner, interacting with them. If we analyse the work done on social networks by institutions, we can see that many of them seek, through the volume of posts, to be present in the daily lives of their followers. Others invest in advertising on the channel itself (to reach more people) in the hope that this will attract loyal followers. In Pref's case, the investment was to try to speak the "language of the Internet" which, according to a survey carried out in Australia[45] , mostly reaches young people and teenagers (who tend to have a pop culture repertoire associated with them).

The posts published by Pref's take on a stripped-down role, using, for the most part, characters that

[45] The research was cited in an article in which a professor from the Federal University of Juiz de Fora (UFJF) answers some questions related to the way young people use writing on the Internet. The article is available at: http://veja.abril.com.br/idade/exdusivo/perguntas respostas/linguagem- Intemet-celular/idioma-escrita-abreviada-jovens-adolescentes.shtml accessed on 20/07/2016

are easily identified by a younger audience that recognises pop culture. This effort to please the users who follow Pref's is nothing more than an attitude aimed at maintaining a constant relationship. Bauman (2004) helps us confirm this idea when he says "there is nothing that promotes a comfortable relationship more than mutual praise" (p.16), in other words, you have to try to please your audience so that they can interact with your posts.

However, this process of gaining attention is continuous, since staying connected to a particular channel is a user's choice. There is volatility in this process, since a simple unsubscribe from[46] means that the user no longer receives posts from a particular page. Therefore, in a relationship process you always have to reinvent yourself, trying to develop new actions and offer new alternatives to keep the user's attention. We realised that these actions are characteristic of any relationship when we saw that

> Affinity is born of choice, and this umbilical cord is never cut. Unless the choice is reaffirmed daily and new actions continue to be taken to confirm it, affinity withers, withers and deteriorates until it disintegrates (BAUMAN, 2004, p.22).

If we think about the digital environment, more specifically social networks, a relationship disintegrates when a company's posts no longer reach their audience. This happens mainly when the content posted doesn't attract the attention of the people who follow a particular page. For this reason, provoking people's participation, which in the case of Facebook means their adherence to a particular post through comments and/or shares, is like an invitation to an ongoing relationship, as described by Bauman (2004) "living together can mean sharing the boat, the rations and the cabin bed. It can mean sailing together and sharing the joys and hardships of the journey" (p. 23). Or sharing content on social networks (Lovemarks).

Pref's has managed to attract the attention of people with different interests. Obviously, the common point of everything they publish is related to the city of Curitiba; however, the page has achieved such success that users from all over Brazil have started to follow it.

The city has reached a much higher number of followers than other capitals that have a significantly larger population than Curitiba. The capital of Paraná has 846,000 likes on its page, while capitals such as São Paulo and Rio de Janeiro, with much larger populations, have 269,000 and 170,000, respectively, according to the graph below (figure 26).

---

[46] In order to follow a company, a user needs to click on a "like" button available on all Facebook pages. The reverse process takes place when this user clicks on "unfollow", thus no longer receiving posts from that page.

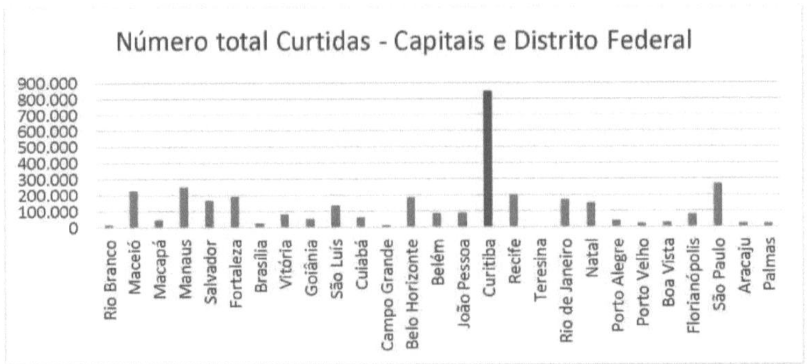

Figure 26 - Graph explaining the big difference in the number of likes between the capitals of all Brazilian states and the federal district
Source: Facebook.com created by the author of the dissertation

Once again, Bauman (2004) helps us to understand how this process takes place when he says:

The only way to include the 'strangers' in a 'we' was to bring them together as potential partners in confessional rituals, tending to reveal a similar (and therefore familiar) 'interior' when pressed to share their intimate sincerities. (BAUMAN, 2004, p. 24)

This shows us that the language of the Internet, especially that related to what we call pop culture in this dissertation, is the one that prevails, since even if they live outside Curitiba, users from all over Brazil recognise and identify messages that have been designed and created with the aim of first attracting people's attention and then transmitting institutional information.

The prominence that Pref's work has achieved in recent years is therefore evident. The success has achieved (measured in number of likes) can be attributed to actions that have gained great national repercussions, such as the case of the Red Wedding, in which Pref's was invited to marry Rio de Janeiro's City Hall[47] . In this episode, several media outlets, such as newspapers and TV news programmes, as well as the publicity on social networks, made Pref's actions reach a greater number of people than the number of active Internet users in the capital of Paraná. Research carried out by FGV/RJ (NERI, 2012) shows that around 71 per cent (approx.
1,256,000 inhabitants at the time of the survey) of Curitiba's population had computers at home. Of this amount, 62 per cent (780,000) had Internet access.

Facebook doesn't provide detailed information by state or capital city; however, according to information from Facebook's director of strategic partnerships, Ime Archibong, presented at Campus Party[48] 2016, 8 out of 10 Brazilians use the social network. If we take this study as a basis, we can deduce that around 620,000 people have access to Facebook in the capital of Paraná. With this data, it's as if we were saying that

---

[47] This action, along with others that make up the corpus of empirical analysis in this research, will be studied separately in the next chapter of this work.
[48] Brazil's main annual technology event. It deals with the most diverse topics related to the Internet, bringing together a large number of communities and users of the World Wide Web involved in technology and digital culture. Available at http://brasil.campus-party.org/ accessed on 25/07/2016

practically everyone who uses the Internet in Curitiba has liked the City Hall page. However, many of these likes come from residents of other cities, who only interacted with the Pref's due to the characteristics of its digital persona (MARK; PEARSON, 2001), the posts that enabled decoding (HALL, 2003) adhering to the repertoire and caused a certain balance in what can be considered legitimate and illegitimate (KOOPMANS, 2004) when it comes to the communication of a public institution.

Of the total number of likes on Pref's page, only 260,000 are from the capital itself, the rest are distributed among other cities as shown in the report (figure 27) .[49]

This process took place mainly due to the large volume of interactions that the published posts garnered. Each post that Pref's made available on its page, using the concepts of legitimacy, visibility and resonance (KOOPMANS, 2004), being faithful to its persona (MARK; PEARSON, 2001) and seeking to develop content that reached people who could recognise that repertoire (NETTO, 1996) caused a decoding (HALL, 2003) that made it possible to achieve a large volume of interactions among those who follow it and, consequently, establish connections that are made up of social ties between the parties that take part in this communication process.

Figure 27 - Data on the distribution of Pref's number of likes by gender, country, city and language - Source Curitiba City Hall Fanpage

3.3 - ABOUT INTERACTIONS

Social networks on the Internet have connections built up through different forms of interaction and social exchange. On the Internet, for example, it is possible to take part in a social group without interacting directly with its members, but only by taking advantage of the information that circulates, as is the case with newsletter subscription lists[50] . It is also possible to interact with a group of bloggers through comments and

[49] Report provided by Pref's team showing the Top 10 cities and countries with the highest number of likes on the page. Source: Curitiba City Hall Fanpage. Updated in June 2016

[50] Companies often offer their public the possibility of subscribing to these lists so that those interested in that

form a social network with them (RECUERO, 2009).

Computer-mediated interactions as formers of social ties can be understood to the extent that these websites and communication systems allow participants to create individualised profiles to interact with each other. On Facebook, a person creates a personal profile and then interacts with other similar profiles, as well as with pages that represent legal entities, such as Pref's. This personalisation is an essential element in forming social bonds. This personalisation is an essential element for establishing interaction, which is anchored in the presence of the other. By building these profiles, the parties can recognise each other as individuals and interact. Recuero (2007) emphasises that these constructions allow the Internet to function as a space for sociability, where social ties can emerge.

Through interactions, social ties are formed that connect the users of a social network. The content of interactions helps characterise a particular social bond. We can see in Pref's actions that the published posts first aim to establish a relationship with their audience and then convey an institutional message, characteristics that we will work on later in this chapter.

Granovetter (1973) categorises social ties as strong and weak. Strong ties are those characterised by a large investment of time, the creation of intimacy, trust and reciprocity. This type of bond seems to be present in the content published by Pref's, since it seeks to gain the trust of its audience in order to then guarantee the message itself. It's as if the people who interact with a particular post belong to that group or network. Mutual interaction constitutes a type of belonging, which can be understood as the feeling that connects the person who publishes a post and their target audience through social ties, making them feel part of the group. Recognising oneself in the context, or at least understanding the context in which the messages were created, contributed to making a connection between the parties.

But, after all, what is the point of establishing a relationship that provokes interactions from the people who follow a particular Facebook page? The channels on which institutional messages were published, for the most part, depended on a considerable financial investment to reach a significant volume of people. In this way, gaining an audience became a mission for those who took over Pref's digital channels: "The department's premise is to conquer media spaces rather than buy them" (BORBA, 2016). Therefore, the relationship becomes a tool, as well as a strategy that has long been developed in marketing, as we discussed at the beginning of this chapter. A tool that aims to attract people to a page, provoking interactions to increase the audience for institutional messages. Before we develop this idea, and even show some examples, we should return to what we discussed in the first chapter of this dissertation with regard to how the social network Facebook works.

The social network's algorithm understands that in order for you to see what is happening with your

---

brand, product or service can frequently receive news, offers and other institutional communications that are made available via email.

"friends", there needs to be an interaction (like, comment or share); if we adopt Recuero's (2009) concept, we can consider these actions as a connection between the parties involved. In this way, the algorithm is able to identify which friends interact with you the most (and vice versa), thus establishing a ranking of posts to be displayed on the user's timeline. Each post that is published receives a score[51] that will determine its degree of exposure. If the score is low, few people will see it. Conversely, if the score is high, the greater the distribution of the post and, consequently, the greater the prominence given to it. Therefore, it is this calculation that determines, based on the relationship that has taken place on the network, which post should appear on people's timelines.

So, if an institution wants its messages to reach a significant audience, it needs to provoke interaction from its users; in practice, posts need to generate the actions of liking, commenting and sharing, the last two of which have greater relevance in the digital relationship process; in other words, commenting on some posts is more valuable than just making a like, just as sharing is worth more than the other two. It is precisely for this reason that Borba (2016) states: "In order to achieve this goal [of reaching a larger audience], we rely on the viralisation potential of the networks in which we operate and we direct all our creative efforts so that the viralisation phenomenon acts on our institutional messages" (2016).

The Pref's team's behaviour has stood out in the digital market precisely because of its innovation in mixing institutional messages with posts aimed at establishing a relationship with its audience. Often, especially for those who don't live in the capital of Paraná, institutional content goes unnoticed, but it is always present in posts. We have selected some of these posts to illustrate how the two proposals (institutional message and relationship) are present in Pref's daily life. In this research, our corpus was limited to posts that took place in 2014; however, in order to exemplify the concepts described in this chapter, we will use more recent posts, which allowed us to better understand the data we want to highlight in terms of the volume of interactions.

The first post we've sorted involves a message informing us about a cold front that was approaching the capital of Paraná in June 2016. The cold wave promised to be one of the most severe in recent years. The City Council's concern was with social issues, since in a city like Curitiba, needy people, homeless people (among others in need) need help to get through the low temperatures that are characteristic of the city. With this in mind, a campaign was created with the aim of sensitising people to donate warm clothes. To contribute and publicise this campaign, Pref's created a post using a pop character from Disney cartoons, Princess Elsa, who in the animation Frozen has special powers and can freeze the things she touches. In the post (figure 28), we see one of the city's parks in the background with the grass covered in frost, and the character Elsa in the foreground. In the description of the post, the message warns of low temperatures in the coming days and, as well as a reference to the cartoon, invites people to take part in the Donate Heat campaign, promoted by the City Council.

---

[51] This is the EdgeRank algorithm. See Chapter 01, p. 13 of this research.

Figure 28- Print of a post published by Curitiba City Hall warning of the intense cold approaching the city Source: Curitiba City Hall Facebook page

If we look at the interactions achieved by this post, we realise that it had a total of 9,600 likes, 453 comments and 2,518 shares. The reach of this post is even greater, since each share appears on the timeline of the user who carried out this action; consequently appearing to all their friends. Based on research published by the Olhar Digital website[52] , on average each Facebook user has 229 friends. This means that this post potentially reached 576,622 people.

Another post we've highlighted features an image that has become famous around the world, especially among music fans. It's the cover of the Beatles' LP in which the band members appear crossing the road at a zebra crossing in front of the Abbey Road Studio office (which eventually gave the album its name). In the post (figure 29), the image was edited and headphones were inserted into the band members. The institutional message was a warning to people to be careful when crossing the road with headphones on. The image was chosen for its connection between music and crossing the street safely. This post received 1,500 likes, 114 shares and 51 comments. Even with the more modest numbers, we can see that a message like this, due to its simplicity (and because it deals with a common subject), would potentially not be covered by more traditional media outlets; however, on social networks it did achieve some repercussion.

[52] Olhar Digital: The average Facebook user has 229 friends, is 38 years old and accesses the social network every day.

Available at: http://olhardigital.uol.com.br/noticia/usuario-medio-do-facebook-tem-229-amigos,-38- years-and-access-social-networking-all-day/22370 . Accessed on 27/07/2016.

Figure 29 - Print of a post published by Curitiba City Hall warning about wearing headphones when crossing the street Source: Curitiba City Hall Facebook page

The last post we'll highlight in these examples uses references from the film Captain America - Civil War. In this film, the character Spider-Man appears in a confrontation with the heroic protagonist, Captain America. Using a passage from the film, Pref's published a post with an image of Captain America in the foreground as his shield is hit by a web produced by Spider-Man. The aim of the post (image 30) was to raise awareness of the brown spider, an arachnid that is common in the capital of Paraná, especially during the summer. There have already been epidemics of this species of spider, which often worries residents and city authorities, as its bite can lead to death. This type of campaign has always been widely publicised in the city. On social media, language aimed at reaching a younger audience (pop culture) was used, achieving 4,500 likes, 313 comments and 446 shares.

Figure 30 - Print of a post published by Curitiba City Hall warning people to beware of brown spiders Source: Curitiba City Hall Facebook page

It's nothing new to say that social networks have brought about major changes in the customer x company relationship. The opportunity to speak directly to those who consume the product or service and, among other things, to give the public immediate feedback have made these channels indispensable for those whose goal is to reach people.

The fact is that companies' communication directly with their customers has become more intense with the use of digital social networks, which have taken on the role of powerful relationship marketing tools, becoming a favourable medium for brands to present their proposals, extol their advantages, exploit all their creative potential to win over the most demanding customer and, above all, test their ability deal with complaints. It's there that people talk most about their dissatisfaction, since this kind of attitude, given the exposure, speeds up possible corrections in order to guarantee the much-desired customer satisfaction. As they become interested in a brand's publication, people naturally spread the word to their friends, which makes them spontaneous multipliers. Doing this via social media apparently makes everything much easier. Anyone who follows a brand on social media is much more than a consumer. They are someone who identifies with and is very interested in what the brand has to say. The consequence of this is the dissemination of content on the web.

Social networks have become significant tools that favour multidirectional communication, in which the speaker (encoder) and interlocutor (decoder) communicate instantaneously by writing about various subjects and expressing their impressions freely and informally, and this content can spread through shares on a digital social network. We can see that, apparently, users of a social network have significant freedom and reach, which can represent opportunities and threats for companies and institutions, as their complaint or praise can be easily located in search engines by consumers interested in certain brands.

In the relationship built up by Pref's, we realise that the team makes a continuous effort to ensure that this channel doesn't become a complaints board. Even though the comments on the posts receive a response from the team, care is taken to always direct the needs to the departments responsible for that particular issue. The strategic proposal is to establish contact with residents so that they work as multipliers of everything that is posted on the Pref's Fanpage.

We can therefore conclude that the digital communication strategies used on social networks, in particular, follow a marketing trend that has been gaining momentum in recent decades. We also realise that it is not easy to establish a relationship with your audience; it is, in fact, a lot of work (not least because of concerns related to decoding (HALL, 2003) and establishing a balance between the legitimate and the illegitimate (KOOPMANS, 2004). Perhaps this explains why institutions are so resistant to adopting this strategy. We have also observed that with the advent of the Internet and social networks, this work has become more accessible and more effective, since many people are present on these channels (and the results of this type of work can be measured through the interactions that take place on each post) in the case of Facebook, for example.

In the next chapter, we will present a case study encompassing three campaigns carried out by Pref's so that we can understand the extent to which this relationship achieves effective results that go beyond a like and/or comment on a post. Our intention in carrying out this case study is to conceptually assess the extent to which the work carried out contributes to achieving concrete results, especially in times of fragile relationships (BAUMAN, 2004).

CHAPTER 4

REALISING RELATIONSHIPS: CASE STUDIES OF ACTIONS TAKEN BY PREF'S

In this research we came across various posts and actions by Pref's. In order to analyse the concepts proposed by this dissertation and their application in terms of implementing actions that go beyond the digital social networking environment, we chose actions by Pref's that involve health-related aspects. We selected these cases because they have characteristics that allow us to establish a process of "humanisation[53] " at Pref's. Let's explain this concept better: the image of a public institution may seem cold and distant from people at first. If we consider the history and perception that common sense has of public organisations, it's not difficult to find opinions that differ from those we've seen in relation to Pref's during the course of this research. This is where we realise the importance of creating a persona, as suggested by Mark and Pearson (2001). In addition, the topic of health enables the process of getting closer to the public by addressing aspects that stimulate and provoke emotion in people (related to maintaining life).

Concern about humanised patient care dates back to the Middle Ages in Europe (MEZZOMO, 2010). After the Renaissance, the administration of hospitals was transferred from religious orders to municipalities, giving rise to an interest in making a profit from health services; but the incurably ill, whether due to illness or lack of means, continued to depend on religious shelters. "You can't humanise an organisation with decrees and regulations. You first bring about a change in people so that you can then change the methods and processes" (SILVA, 2010, p. 215) to form a virtuous spiral in favour of the citizen. Thus, addressing the issue of health in posts that aim to establish a concrete relationship with the people who follow Pref's will allow us to see how the concepts developed during this dissertation are applied in everyday practice beyond the digital social network.

In order to discuss the case study method, three aspects must be considered: the nature of the experience as a phenomenon to be investigated, the knowledge to be achieved and the possibility of generalising studies based on the method. In the case study method, the emphasis is on understanding, based basically on tacit knowledge that has a strong connection with intentionality, which does not occur when the objective is merely explanation, based on propositional knowledge (BECKER, 1997). Thus, when explanation, or the search for propositional knowledge, is the "soul" of a study, the case study can be a disadvantage, but when the objective is understanding, broadening experience, the disadvantage disappears (CESAR, 2005 p. 02).

In the academic environment, particularly in the areas of social science teaching, the use of the case study method can involve both single-case and multiple-case study situations (YIN, 2001). The precautions

[53] This subject will be returned to at the end of this chapter. Even though the humanisation of an institution is unlikely, the importance that Pref's gives to the term is relevant to this dissertation, and we can link it directly to the choice of cases that will be analysed in this chapter.

that must be taken when using multiple cases refer to two fundamental issues: firstly, the sampling criteria, since in studies of this nature the choice of sample is not based on the incidence of phenomena, but rather on the interest of the case in relation to the phenomenon under study and the potentially relevant variables; secondly, the number of cases selected is also related to the theoretical replications necessary for the study, in other words, the certainty that is required, and not to statistical criteria related to significance levels.It can be said that case studies have some characteristics in common: they are complex and holistic descriptions of a reality, involving sets of data; the data is basically obtained through personal observation; the reporting style is informal, narrative, and includes illustrations, allusions and metaphors; the comparisons made are more implicit than explicit; the themes and hypotheses are important, but are subordinate to understanding the case. As an application possibility, a case study goes beyond telling a story: it can be used to test hypotheses, for example, to test the falsifiability of theories:

> a scientific investigation that investigates a contemporary phenomenon within its real-life context, especially when the boundaries between the phenomenon and the context are not clearly defined; faces a technically unique situation in which there will be many more variables of interest than data points and, as a result, draws on multiple sources of evidence (...) and benefits from the prior development of theoretical propositions to conduct data collection and analysis (YIN, 2001, p. 32-33).

To this end, we have selected three cases that were campaigns devised by Pref's team in which we can analyse the results obtained, as well as relate them to the theoretical framework presented in the previous chapters. These cases were chosen because they dealt with issues related to the health of the people involved in the campaigns.

In this way, we can analyse the participation of Pref's followers in the "calls" proposed in the campaigns, the main feature of which is to summon people to donate blood and bone marrow.

We were able to see from this research that Pref's has succeeded in establishing a relationship with the public that follows it on digital channels. It seems that people follow the posts because of a coincidence of repertoire based on the proposed language. As mentioned earlier in this dissertation, this relationship process has attracted fans from all regions of Brazil, thus suggesting a wide reach for the content proposed by the Pref's team.

However, the question about this success and how it can provide some kind of result in effective, concrete actions beyond digital interactions has always been present in this research. After all, the communication process doesn't always follow the path desired by the message encoder (HALL, 2003). Even with the possible interpretations, when considering the preferred reading, it is hoped that the receiver will be able to understand as much as possible of the message as it was intended. If we analyse actions proposed by institutions such as Curitiba City Hall, we can suggest that the end of this communication process, which involves relationships, is the completion of an action. A

> Communicative reason is not only built logically, but first and foremost in the

> processuality of debate. It involves existential decisions, acting in the world and an ethic of solidarity against suffering and oppression. It is a political model in which praxis and words are in deep synergy (DESLANDES; MITRE, 2009, p.643).

As described by the authors, practice has to be in synergy with theory; in other words, when a campaign is published we understand that the expected result is the realisation of an action.

In order to understand a possible realisation of action, we selected three campaigns carried out by Pref's in 2014/2015 to illustrate the hypothesis that relationships can contribute to the realisation of a communication process, through the realisation of actions proposed by Pref's.

4.1 - RED WEDDING

In September 2014, Pref's was already gaining followers on the digital social networks on which it operated. This success brought unusual interactions with the posts published, such as several marriage proposals made by fans of the page to Pref's. A curious situation, since it doesn't seem to make sense for an individual to propose to a public institution. A curious situation, since it doesn't seem to make sense for an individual to propose to a public institution. This suggests that, at that point, Pref's had already developed its persona in such a way that proposing would be a way of showing admiration for the content developed and published by the Pref's team. The requests came from individuals, i.e. followers of the page, but also from a public institution. Among the various requests, the one from Rio de Janeiro City Hall caught the team's attention due to the interactions with that post (figure 31).

Figure 31 Post in which Rio's city hall suggests a wedding. Source: Curitiba City Hall FanPage

The Pref's fan page then began to receive several comments encouraging this "union". From this acceptance (due to the large volume of interactions) from the page's followers, an exchange of messages suggesting a process of acquaintance between the two town halls, a kind of courtship between them, took over the Pref's Facebook page.

The unusual request gained space in the traditional media, which reported on the union process. We realise here the importance of circulation between traditional media and digital social networks. We'll address this issue a little later in this analysis.

Five days after the first invitation from Rio de Janeiro City Hall, the Prefs then accepted the request (figure 32), thus starting a joint campaign between the two public institutions that became known as the Red Wedding, a name chosen in reference to a sequence from an episode of the Game of Thrones series[54] . Paradoxically, in the TV series the context of the Red Wedding involved great violence, death and blood, while Pref's action was aimed at donating blood to preserve life.

Figure 32 - Post in which Pref's accepts the marriage proposal

Source: Curitiba City Hall FanPage

A brief separate comment on the sequence is in order, since its importance justifies the use of the reference for Pref's campaign. We're not going to contextualise the entire series here, not least because the passage in question takes place at the end of the third season, so it's difficult to explain the importance of characters and the plot itself that have been highlighted so far in this text. The sequence shows a betrayal by

father of the bride who was to marry one of the series' protagonists. The betrayal was considered shocking because, at the behest of the father, the groom (protagonist), the bride (his own daughter) and the groom's mother (another protagonist) were brutally murdered during the wedding celebration and in a way that was

[54] Game of Thrones is an American television series created by David Benioff and D.B. Weiss for HBO. The series is based on the book series The Song of Ice and Fire, written by George R. R. Martin, with its title being derived from the first book. The reference to the name Red Wedding was inspired by the sequence that ended episode 9 of the third season, whose original title is The Rains of Castamere, but was given the name The "Red Wedding" by fans of the series. Available at: http://gameofthrones-brasiLbtogspot.com.br/2013/06/a-importancia-do-casamento- vermelho-em.html Accessed on 15/10/2016. The sequel can be watched at: https://www.youtube.com/watch?v=DQsl5Bz312k.

completely unexpected by the series' followers. The event provoked many reactions and comments. However, the episode shocked people around the world so much that several videos of their reactions as they watched it spread across digital social networks .[55]

Here we see the use of repertoire as a way of creating audience identification with the episode, as well as the paradoxical reference to blood donation, which ended up being the main reason for the whole action. Returning to the context presented earlier in this dissertation, repertoire is understood as "a kind of vocabulary, a stock of signs known and used by an individual" (NETTO, 1996, p.123). In this way, the quest to create an area of repertoire that coincides with the public following Pref's Facebook page is seen as a digital marketing strategy to attract and engage people with the proposed content. This consideration is justified since this approach is present in most of the posts we have shown in this dissertation and is possibly present in this campaign. The results obtained in posts where there is a repertoire recognised by the target audience are potentially greater. Of course, not everyone who came into contact with the campaign directly recognised the reference to the Game of Thrones series. However, using something that has moved digital networks (the episode in which the Red Wedding took place aired in December 2013) could improve the results desired with the action.

If we analyse the post itself (image 32) that Pref's published with the message "Its Mach", it already gives us a basis for reaffirming the importance of repertoire in the coding of messages, since this image comes from the Tinder app[56] to indicate when two people who have met through the app have a mutual interest in each other.

The campaign was then planned so that followers of the page could be invited to this union, thus contributing to a social action proposed by the two town halls. As the main objective, it was suggested that guests give the "bride and groom" a blood donation as a gift (figure 33).

[55] A publication with several of these videos with people's reactions can be found at this address: http://hojeemdia.com.br/opini%C3%A3o/blogs/box-1.8052/confira-as-rea%C3%A7%C3%B5es-de-f%C3%A3s-de- game-of-thrones-ao-assistirem-%C3%A0-cena-do-casamento-vermelho-1.368772 Acesso em 15/10/2016.

[56] The application is used by people looking for partners in digital social networking environments. In practice, users select people they are interested in meeting. When the interest of one of these people is reciprocated, the application then signals with the expression **it's match**, thus opening up communication between these people. More information can be found at: https://www. gotinder.com/press Accessed on 21/10/2016

Figure 33 - Red wedding invitation post Source: Curitiba City Hall FanPage

As noted above, it is worth analysing the participation of the traditional media in covering the event. The "wedding" process had already been closely followed by traditional channels that reported on the union of the two city halls (ANNEX I, p 18). In the post above (figure 33) we can see that RPC (Rede Paranaense de Comunicação, Rede Globo's affiliate in Paraná) was indicated as the master of ceremonies for the event. This makes us reflect on the integration between online and offline as a way of ensuring a greater reach of people. Even though in a digital environment there is a large circulation of people, using the support of a local TV station contributed to the success of the campaign in which it is possible to observe a continuum between online and offline. Curiously, even though it was considered the master of ceremonies, RPC didn't cover the action in stories that aired on TV news programmes; it mainly followed up on the broadcaster's digital channels[57] . On the other hand, other broadcasters, such as BAND Curitiba, did a story[58] about the action that aired on the local news programme BAND Cidade Curitiba.

In addition to the proposal to donate blood, companies from the capital of Paraná were interested in taking part in the action. Seeking to get more people involved, Pref's then created its wedding list in which it asked companies (or even individuals) to do good deeds for the city of Curitiba in celebration of the union of the two capitals. This list[59] contained 11 items that could be chosen by companies. They were asked to: 1 - Take 50 children to the cinema and 50 children to the theatre; 2 - Donate 100 books to municipal schools and 100 books to the tuboteca[60] ; 3 - Clean 20 graffitied walls; 4 - 1 graffiti commemorating the union between the

[57] As an example, here are two articles published by the digital channels G1 Paraná and Gazeta do Povo On-line, respectively, linked to the RPC group, which reported on the action: http://g1.globo.com/pr/parana/noticia/2014/09/casamento-das-prefs-alavanca-doacao-de-sangue-em-curitiba.html Accessed on 21/10/2016. http://www.gazetadopovo.com.br/vida-e-cidadania/casamento-virtual-between-curitiba-and-rio-de-janeiro-stimulates-social-actions-ee1h1zn21omi2skgxsf3f9cni Accessed on 21/10/2016

[58] Available at https://www.youtube.com/watch?v=JJnho5n2EUA accessed on 21/10/2016

[59] Available at: http://bandnewsfmcuritiba.com/casamento-da-prefeitura-de-curitiba-mobiliza-empresas- and-blood-donors-this-saturday Accessed on 21/09/2016

[60] Libraries at the city's bus stops, which are known as tube stations because of their physical shape.

cities; 5 - Recreational activities for patients in a general hospital and a children's hospital; 6 - Plant 321 trees; 7 - Provide a sightseeing tour of the city for a group of senior citizens; 8 - Creating an action to restore the self-esteem of women who have been victims of violence; 9 - Employment or training for 50 people with disabilities and 50 socially vulnerable citizens; 10 - Distributing 150 popsicles to workers exposed to the sun; 11 - Posting on the internet the drawings of 100 children about their city in the future.

As a result of the action, there were record blood donations in the cities involved. In the capital of Paraná, the haemobank (the city's main collection point) used up its maximum number of donations in one day (300) (APPENDIX 1, p.24). Other collection points were opened in Curitiba to cope with the large influx of people joining the campaign. Queues for donations were recorded at all the collection points, a situation that is not seen on regular operating days. Responsible for supplying blood to all the hospitals of Rio de Janeiro's Municipal Health Department, Hemorio carried out 225 collections, 30% more than normal[61] . In addition to the donations themselves, a number of companies joined the list of gifts, carrying out Pref's requests aimed at creating social actions around the city. For example, a local bar, Bossa Nova bar, distributed popsicles and water to street workers, the São José dos Pinhais Shopping Centre (located in the city of the same name, in the metropolitan region of Curitiba) took children to the cinema, and the Halpar Company planted 321 araucaria trees around the city (APPENDIX 1, p. 21). Clearly, the companies and other participants in this action took advantage of the situation so that their brands could be linked to the campaign which, at that moment, was already attracting the attention of people all over Brazil.

In total, the campaign reached 3,192,512[62] people through the posts published on Facebook. This does not include the reach provided by the various articles published in newspapers and magazines throughout Brazil. We can understand that the action may have been responsible for the large reach of people that Pref's has achieved, especially outside the city of Curitiba, thus explaining the success and large number of likes registered on the fanpage.

Even with these considerations, the process of analysing this case is complex and involves a number of reflections. The first is the perception of mobilisation, which took place through various media outlets and not just Pref's profile on the digital social network. People responded to Pref's "call" and went to donate blood to take part in the action. It's curious to note that what caught the attention of the people who joined the campaign was the marriage between two institutions, a fact unlikely to be realised in practice, but in a digital social network environment, it was not only possible, but the celebration of this process culminated in blood donations.

The research carried out in this dissertation allows us to relate the expressive reach of this campaign to the concept of resonance described by Koopmans (2004). We understand that the process of a union between two capitals causes a balance between what can be called highly legitimate and highly illegitimate. We

[61] Available at: http://www.rio.rj.gov.br/web/guest/exibeconteudo?id=4983423 accessed on 08/10/2016
[62] Figures provided by the Pref's team, available in Appendix 1 of this dissertation.

consider the idea of creating a social campaign between two cities that could engage people in favour of a cause related to health and well-being to be legitimate. On the other hand, we could consider a marriage between two public institutions to be illegitimate, an action that is impossible given that this type of liaison involves the union of two city halls (an institutional partnership would be possible, but not a marriage). The balance between these two concepts (adhering to the campaign, but finding the union unusual) enabled the action to have great resonance, not only on the digital social networks in which the two town halls operate, but also in the traditional media coverage of the event, reporting on what happened and also contributing to the success of the campaign by taking on the role of master of ceremonies (RPC).

We can say, from observations made as a resident of the capital of Paraná, that campaigns calling for blood donations are frequent and use traditional communication channels (radio, TV, printed newspapers, etc.). However, there are no reports of people exceeding the daily limit, as happened on the day of the Red Wedding.

In this way, we also observed that the Red Wedding allowed the message to take part in a circulation process (HALL, 2003), since its proposal was translated into a context in which people sought to identify with it through a repertoire (Game of Thrones, Tinder), a story that involved people's emotional aspects (after all, weddings are a time when people become more sensitive) and, assuming that the proposed message was translated into a social event that aimed, firstly, to involve people in the action, so that they would then take action (donating blood); we can conclude that the process of realising the action was a consequence of the people involved being able to decode the message in the way it was planned, or, as described by Hall (2003), in a dominant hegemonic position, in which the decoder assimilates the meaning in the way it was referentially coded in the production process.Generally speaking, it is possible to deduce that the relationship established between Pref's and its followers enabled the campaign to achieve success (a large number of blood donors). The relationship we are referring to takes place from the acceptance of the marriage proposal, since we can consider that the "pressure" of the fans of the page who followed the proposal was present, to the realisation of the action, breaking the record for daily blood donations in both Curitiba and Rio de Janeiro, which register an average of 150 [63] daily donations on regular days.

4.2 - Enzo Day

On 12 February 2014, through its Facebook message box, Curitiba City Hall received an alert about the need for bone marrow donations at the city's banks, in an attempt to save the boy Enzo (who has Fanconi

[63] Here's a news item from Curitiba's local newspaper about blood donations in 2016, which records the average quoted in the text. Available at: http://g1.globo.com/pr/parana/noticia/2016/09/hemepar-pede-para-populacao-doar-sangue-antes-do-feriado-prolongado.html accessed on 17/10/2016. In the case of Rio de Janeiro, we mentioned earlier in this chapter that the campaign increased the number of donors by around 30 per cent. Since the campaign's total number of collections was 225, if we deduct the 30 per cent increase, we arrive at a figure of around 150, which was mentioned in the text.

Anaemia[64] and is a fan of superheroes). As part of the mobilisation, the Pref's made posts related to the case asking citizens to register as donors at the Hemobanco. The image was published and shared thousands of times (ANNEX 1, p 5). The day after it was published, there was a queue of over an hour and a half waiting to donate blood (as seen in the post shown in figure 34)

Figure 34 - Post highlighting the number of people donating blood for young Enzo Source: Curitiba City Hall FanPage

Despite the mobilisation, the young man, who had already undergone two bone marrow transplants, was unable to resist the progression of the disease and died. As a way of honouring him, a campaign was devised that became known as Enzo Day (figure 35), dedicated to registering new bone marrow donors. The campaign had great repercussions, reaching other localities such as the city of São Paulo, which also opened a collection point (figure 36).

As a final result, the campaign reached around 800,000[65] people in all the posts published on the subject; it obtained 315 new registrations of bone marrow donors, which represents a record for this type of donation since during a regular donation month no more than 450 donations are counted[66] . In addition, the campaign was extended for another year (2015), also involving a large number of donors and thousands of people (ANNEX 1, p14).

---

[64] Fanconi anaemia (FA) is an inherited DNA repair disease characterised by progressive pancytopenia with bone marrow failure, variable congenital malformations and a predisposition to haematological or solid tumours. The disease causes the destruction of the bone marrow, preventing it from producing new blood cells for the body to function normally. Fanconi anaemia also causes the bone marrow to produce many defective blood cells, causing serious health problems such as leukaemia, which affected young Enzo. Available at: http://www.orpha.net/consor/cgi-bin/OC_Exp.php?Lng=EN&Expert=84 Accessed on 22/09/2016

[65] Figures provided by the Pref's team, available in Appendix 1 of this dissertation.

[66] Available at: http://g1.globo.com/pr/parana/noticia/2014/02/campanha-para-doacao-de-medula- ossea-leva-315-pessoas-ao-hemepar.html Accessed on 15/10/2016

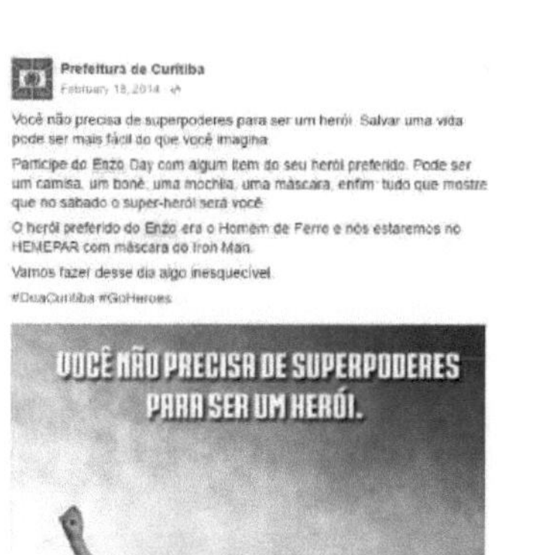

Figura 35 - Postagem convocando para o Enzo Day
Fonte: FanPage da Prefeitura Municipal de Curitiba

Figura 36 - Postagem confirmando a participação da cidade de São Paulo
Fonte: FanPage da Prefeitura Municipal de Curitiba

Figure 35 - Post calling for Enzo Day Source: Curitiba City Hall FanPage
Figure 36 - Post confirming the participation of the city of São Paulo Source: Curitiba City Hall FanPage

We also saw a link between this campaign and the concepts discussed in this dissertation. Once again, the search for identity with the target audience through repertoire is evident, since the approach to identifying the character, Enzo, related the young man to the comic book character Iron Man[67] . One of the images posted by the youngster's mum showed Enzo dressed in an Iron Man costume. From then on, the reference to the comic book character was present in most of the posts.

In addition to this reference, we can also see the presence of the symbolism of the "amateur" superhero in the post calling for the campaign (figure 35). In the text that says: "You don't need superpowers to be a superhero", we can see the attempt to convey the idea that, by helping with the campaign, anyone could act as if they were a superhero. The very image chosen (a boy wearing a "homemade" cape and mask) refers to this issue. The image of a child playing at being a superhero conveys, in our view, both the idea that anyone can take on the role of a hero and also provokes emotion in people that a child who always wanted to be a superhero needed help and didn't get it in time. Thus, the message was constructed in such a way as to impact people through emotional aspects, putting the message into circulation.

Still in relation to this scenario, we would highlight the text contained in image 34, which calls on

[67] He is one of the world's best-known superheroes, created by Marvel Comics. In addition to the comics and a series of Iron Man films, the character is also the protagonist of another series, The Avangers. The sequels were released in 2008 (Iron Man) and 2012 (The Avangers). Both sequels were very successful, especially among Brazilian children and young adults. (Available at https://pt.wikipedia.org/wiki/Homem_de_Ferro accessed on 19/10/2016.

followers with the following line: "The social network being used for GOOD". Who better to do good than a superhero? This way, the relationship between the post and the search for an identity, a repertoire, is also present in this action.

The second concept that we relate to action is the process of circulating information (HALL, 2003). In order for a message to be decoded according to the plan of the person who encoded it, it needs to be inserted into an information circuit: (i) Production - The message is planned in such a way as to try and assign some meaning to it. In the Enzo Day campaign, as well as the approach offering a significant emotional appeal, because it was about a child with a rare disease, the construction of the message used elements related to the day-to-day life of the boy Enzo, who lived in costume as a superhero[68] . Because of this, the campaign used as a reference an image posted by Enzo's mother, in which the youngster appeared in an Iron Man costume (Figure 37).

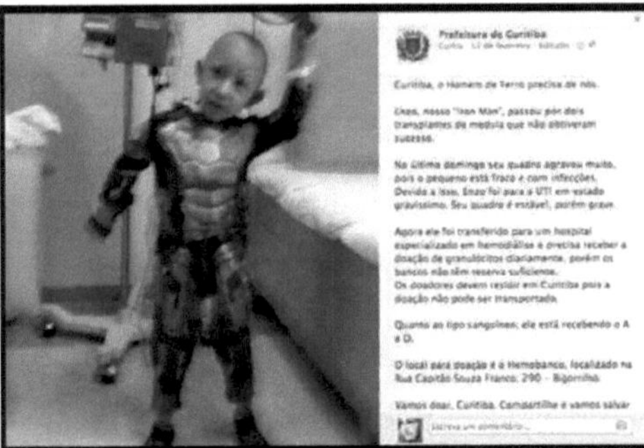

Figure 37 - Posting by young Enzo's hand and shared by Pref's Source: Curitiba City Hall FanPage

This image was shared by Pref's with the phrase: "Iron Man needs us", thus gaining more followers, since people seemed motivated to help that child who was fighting for his life. In this way, the message took on a new meaning which, in our view, aimed to move and impact people so that they would join the campaign. (ii) Circulation - The original message, published by Enzo's mum, gained traction on the web because it was about a topic that usually moves people. The idea of using a social network for this type of action is quite common, but it wasn't until Pref's replicated the message that the campaign began to take off; (iii) Consumption and Distribution - The large number of people who followed Pref's at the time took up the call of a mother seeking the best for her son; Thus, the message reached even more people; (iv) Reproduction - Those who followed the campaign began to reach out to more people, seeking the engagement of friends and family in favour of a child they didn't know, but who was already winning over fans who were moved by his story.

We also analysed in this action that the concept of legitimacy and resonance (KOOPMANS, 2004) can be present as we observed that the fact that a child is at imminent risk of death from a disease related to

[68] In the images published of young Enzo, it was common to see him dressed up as a superhero such as the aforementioned Iron Man, Captain America or even just wearing an improvised astronaut helmet, as can be seen in the article http://g1.globo.com/pr/parana/noticia/2014/02/campanha-para- doacao-de-medula-ossea-leva-315-pessoas-ao-hemepar.html Accessed 19/10/2016.

cancer could be considered highly illegitimate (because it is something unexpected, unusual, out of the norm); on the other hand, an action that encourages bone marrow donation is highly legitimate, but does not always impact people. Thus, telling the story of a young man, a "little superhero", seems to strike a balance between these two poles, favouring the message to resonate and reach a greater number of people.

Once again, we can highlight the support of traditional media outlets (COBERTURA, 2016) for the action proposed by the Pref's. However, the agenda for this coverage was apparently due to the great repercussions that the case had on social networks, a concept that we can relate to the Melding Agenda, discussed earlier in this dissertation, which occurs when individuals participate in groups and "merge" their personal agendas with the agenda of a group. Thus, we can understand that the repercussions initiated in a social network environment, and referenced by traditional media outlets, led to significant numbers of bone marrow donations, thus leading us to conclude that the action was realised through the relationship established on Pref's page.

4.3 - Rare Blood Donor - Marli Wanted

The last case selected could be considered the simplest, if we think about the production of a campaign: unlike the other cases discussed in this chapter, Pref's didn't actually produce or design a campaign. The process happened spontaneously with a request for help from a blood donation institute, Hemepar, which needed to locate a resident of the city of Curitiba and asked Pref's to publish a call for help on its Facebook page. The simplicity stops there. What would have been just a call became a reference due to the efficiency and quick results that the post on the digital social network provided.

The story begins with the Belo Horizonte - MG haemobank looking for a blood type with very rare[69] antigens for a patient in the capital of Minas Gerais who was in a serious condition. A alert for this demand was issued to haemobanks across the country. In Paraná, it was detected that there was only one donor with this type of blood in the Curitiba database. Hemepar therefore asked the city council for help in trying to find the donor, Marli Aparecida da Silva. As soon as it received Hemepar's request, Pref's launched a post (figure 38) looking for Mrs Marli.

---

[69] On the surface of each of our red blood cells, there are up to 342 antigens - these are molecules capable of triggering the production of specialised proteins called antibodies. It is the presence or absence of specific antigens that determines a person's blood type. Around 160 of the blood group 342 antigens are "high prevalence, which means that they are found in the red blood cells of most people. If you don't have an antigen that 99 per cent of people in the world have, your blood is considered rare. Now if you don't have one that 99.99 per cent of people have, then you have very rare blood. Available at: http://www.mundobiologia.com/2014/10/conheca-a-historia-do-homem-com-o-sangue-de-ouro.html#ixzz4NBzjH1xZ accessed on 15/10/2016

Figure 38 - Post looking for Marli - donor of a very rare type of blood Source: Curitiba City Hall FanPage

In less than an hour, Marli was found. The post reached more than 1 million people. More than 9,000 shares of the message meant that the patient from Minas Gerais was able to receive the rare blood and have her life saved thanks to a national mobilisation and, above all, the power of propagability that Pref's was able to impose on the case. Propagation is often used in digital social networks in cases of sharing or commenting, showing consumer engagement and also potential audiences, who perceive certain content as relevant to share with other members of a platform. In the propagability effect, subjects make decisions before propagating content on the network, as well as having the ability to assign a new meaning to the message even before sharing it on their digital social networks. Therefore, the act of propagating does not imply a passive interactor, but a fully active interactor, who will propagate a discourse that is significant to them and if it is not completely significant to them, they can make it so, based on a discursive (re)appropriation (JENKINS; GREEN; FORD, 2014). In this action, it seems clear that the phenomenon of propagability is present, as we realise the intention of people to transmit this message with the aim of finding the donor in question, thus contributing to the success of the campaign.

We would also highlight the symbolism present in the image created (figure 38). There are two symbols that can only be understood by those with the right repertoire. In the first, we see an icon that is normally used to suggest the location of something on a map (it's a red balloon, with the black dot in the centre that is usually used on Google maps).

Thus, the suggested reading of this image is to find a location for something (or someone). In the same image, on the opposite side, we see another balloon that symbolises, in our interpretation, a drop of blood, thus suggesting the donation that the campaign intended. Santaella (2003) offers us an explanation that we can relate to analysing the image: "a sign is something that represents another sign" (p.12); in the case of figure 38, the image of the locator also refers to a drop of blood, promoting a kind of mutual inference.

We also see a relationship that can be analysed in this action from the perspective of Koopmans' theory (2004). After all, a person needing a very rare blood type for which there is only one catalogued compatible donor in the whole country seems unlikely (highly illegitimate). On the other hand, the search for a rare blood donor who could save someone else's life can be considered a highly legitimate action. In this case, identifying the rare donor and launching a search via a digital social network provided the necessary balance to achieve the appropriate resonance that allowed the donor to be found. This case also allows us to infer that Pref's, at the time, had participatory followers who felt part of the search process. The post (figure 39) announcing that Marli had been found carries not only information about the success of an action, but also thanks to everyone who got involved and contributed to the satisfactory end result.

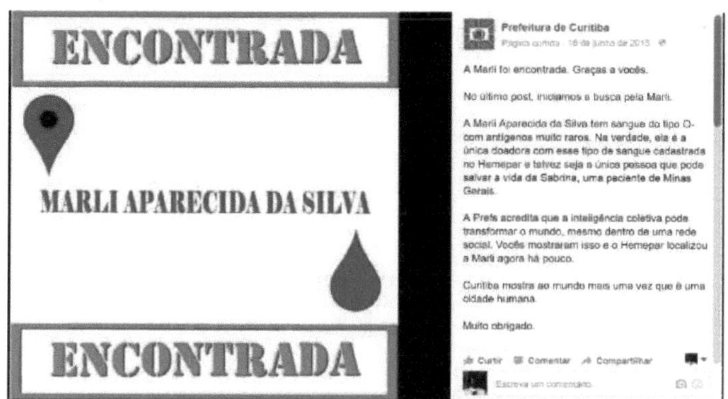

Figure 39 - Thank you post for mobilising to find Marli Source: Curitiba City Hall FanPage

We think that this process is only possible through an established relationship in which people want to help, not just because they are part of the process, but because they want to help someone they care about; in this case Pref's. In the post above, the text mentions collective intelligence: "Pref's believes that collective intelligence can change the world", referring to Pierre Levy's (2000) concept of collective intelligence:

> collective intelligence is not an exclusively cognitive concept. Intelligence should be understood here as in the expression 'working in common agreement... an intelligence distributed everywhere, ceaselessly valued, coordinated in real time that results in an effective mobilisation of competences... The basis and objective of collective intelligence is the mutual recognition and enrichment of people and not the cult of fetishised or hypostatised communities. (p. 26-29)

The author argues that all individuals have their own intelligence accumulated in their personal experiences. He reiterates that it serves as a mode of social interaction, as it is capable of creating a kind of real-time democracy, given its constant possibilities for interaction between peers. In our view, this is exactly what the text highlighted above refers to. It seems that the speed with which the case was resolved resembles an action between friends, who spare no effort or time to help those they love. Something like a call made by Pref's that was answered by his followers/friends. The best evidence of this process is the fact that the need to find the rare donor did not come directly from Pref's, but from Hemepar (the organisation responsible for blood collection). Hemepar, in turn, asked for Pref's help to create the campaign, which, due to the reach Pref's already had at the time, could be successfully concluded through collective intelligence, according to Levy (2000).

Thus, these cases allow us to understand how Pref's brought about a change in the way residents of

Curitiba, and other cities too, perceived the institution during the years 2014/2015. At that time, the actions proposed in Pref's daily routine allowed more people to follow and take an interest in what was happening in the city.

We realised that although the communication channel is new and requires a different approach to reach people, what Pref's uses is a concept that

> can be understood as Public Communication, insofar as it is an instrument for building the public agenda and directs its work towards accountability, stimulating the population's engagement in the policies adopted, recognising the actions promoted in the political, economic and social fields, in short, provoking public debate. It is a legitimate way for a government to render accounts and bring to the attention of public opinion the projects, actions, activities and policies it carries out that are in the public interest. (BRANDÃO, 2005)

In addition, people's engagement with the Facebook page gave those who followed it the chance to start exercising what could culminate in a form of citizenship[70] , as their participation in the proposed actions took place.

To this end, we concluded that there was a satisfactory realisation of actions due to people seeking to establish a link with the institution they were already following digitally. The process of joining a campaign makes citizens an active part of the process of participation and social engagement. What Pref's achieved through its actions in digital environments was to establish a close relationship with its public, reducing the traditional institutional distance that apparently kept citizens away from city affairs.

Perhaps this is the point that was intended when it is quoted in the final post (figure 39): "Curitiba shows the world once again that it is a human city". We know that it's impossible for a city to be humane. Its residents can act in a more humane and civilised way. This premise of making the city "more human" is part of a digital communication strategy recognised by professionals in the field. According to Rafael Terra[71] (2014), in Pref's case, this "humanisation" took place through various actions, especially those involving solidarity. In this way, we understand that Pref's role with this action was to provide this feeling to its residents, from the point that living in a city that calls itself humane (as strange as that may sound) also makes you a more participative human being.

---

[70] Starting from Aristotle's concept and definition of citizen, which says: "a citizen is one who participates in the powers of the state". In other words, to be a member of the political community it is not enough to live in a country (or city). It is essential to have effective power to intervene in the state (ARISTÓTELES, 2002).

[71] Rafael terra is CEO of Fabulosa Ideia. MBA lecturer. Speaker and consultant on Digital Marketing and Brand Humanisation. Available at: https://br.linkedin.com/in/rafaelterraoficial . In an interview with RádioWeb, the professor comments on Pref's work on social networks, especially in terms of the process of what he calls humanising Pref's brand. The interview can be seen at: https://www.youtube.com/watch?v=L3FsDhIQ5G0 Accessed on 21/10/2016.

CHAPTER 5

FINAL CONSIDERATIONS

The development of this dissertation provided a series of reflections that went beyond those idealised at the start of the Master's course. Naturally, the initial plans for this research were moulded as new knowledge, authors and concepts were introduced. At first, there was a personal concern associated with writing a scientific paper, since, as already mentioned in the Introduction to this dissertation, my field of work is much more related to the labour market than to academia. However, the possibility of conceptually analysing everyday situations proved to be a challenge that undoubtedly contributed to my development.

Using a "case" that had stood out on the digital social networking scene and starting an analysis process that sought to understand, through a theoretical basis, how it was possible for the analysed object to achieve such success was gratifying and, at the same time, surprising, as we were able to see how communicational concepts are effectively present in the actions developed by Pref's.

It was possible to see that the content production team was not just made up of a group of young people who had been put in charge of the digital social networks of a public institution; nor were they professionals who had no knowledge of the subject. I admit that, at first, this was the perception we had, because some civil servants are labelled as not being able to dedicate themselves satisfactorily to their duties because they are not specialists in the job, and they are often moved from department to department according to party political changes in a town hall.

In the case of Pref's, the department was set up under the responsibility of a secretariat, which according to Borba (20116) had the mission of innovation, a premise that was pointed out as a characteristic of the management of the then mayor of Curitiba .[72]

> The willingness to innovate opened up space for cheap and innovative ideas to be presented. Each area contributed to this in its own way. The collaboration of the Social Communication Secretariat was the creation of our department; the Internet and Social Media Department. (BORBA, 2016)

If it was under the responsibility of a secretariat, it would then be subject to any changes in government, as the secretaries of a town hall are part of the commissioned staff, appointed by the current mayor, and may or may not undergo changes during the government in which they were appointed, or in any succession[73] . In any case, the Internet and Social Media Department was created and, in its constitution, professionals from the communications area were part of the first team, thus bringing to the environment of a

---

[72] Gustavo Fruet served as mayor of Curitiba between January 2013 (the year Pref's was created) and December 2016.

[73] This survey was completed in 2016, the year of the mayoral elections. On this occasion, Mayor Gustavo Fruet failed to win re-election. However, it has not yet been possible to determine whether there will be changes with the Pref's, since the dissertation was completed before the new mayor took office.

public institution a marketing vision that had a very clear objective:

> The department's premise is to win media space instead of buying it, saving resources on media buying. In order to achieve this goal, we rely on the viralisation potential of the networks in which we operate and we direct all our creative efforts so that the phenomenon of viralisation acts on our institutional messages. (BORBA, 2016)

At this point we can already conclude that the process that Borba (2016) calls viralisation is, in fact, the phenomenon of Propagability. The use of the term 'viral' is much more linked to the team's marketing approach than to the theoretical context of differentiating between viralisation and propagability. However, our aim is to bring a more scientific perspective to a marketing approach and, in this context, the difference exists and needs to be emphasised. Shenja van der Graaf apud Jenkins; Green; Ford, (2014) states that "the main aspect of viral marketing is that it relies heavily on interconnected peers" (p. 36). Thus, the message is transmitted from one peer to another without any kind of audience participation other than spreading the message. On the other hand, propagability depends on the participation of the parties; in other words, it actually occurs when the public interacts with the content. Jenkins; Green; Ford, (2014) attribute propagability to a new model in which

> the public plays an active role in the 'propagation' of content, rather than just serving as a passive carrier of viral media: their choices, their investments, their interests and purposes, as well as their actions, determine what gains value (p. 37).

In this way, we were able to conclude in this research that Pref's makes use of propagability, since the participation of the page's followers is active, allowing people to interact with the content published, and also in the adherence to campaigns devised by the Pref's team in order to attract the participation of residents.

The process of establishing a relationship with people through a digital social network depends on people following a particular channel. Therefore, since Pref's was created in 2013 and had not been active on digital social networks before then, it was necessary to establish a strategy to reach a greater number of people so that they would contribute to the propagation of Pref's proposed messages. In this way, we identified 3 factors that we consider to be fundamental for analysing the hypothesis related to the implementation of proposed actions through digital social networks raised in this research.

The first factor that helped Pref's establish a bond with its public was the creation of a persona. It was necessary to break away from the paradigm of a cold public institution, distant from the people, which used its communication channels only to inform and not to relate. The search for an identity that is recognised and respected on the web is not an easy task; however, for Pref's, the process occurred spontaneously and with the participation of the people. The posting of a warning against a storm in which followers commented "dementadores" is considered by us to be a "watershed" in the communication process established by Pref's on its digital social network. In our analysis, the unfolding of this post (as an example, we highlight the post patronum do cavalo babão) allowed Pref's to then assume his personality (identified by us as the archetypes of the Prestativo and the Bobo da Corte (MARK; PEARSON, 2001)) which would be present in most of his posts from then on. Using the reference to archetypes, we can also infer that Pref's has the Hero archetype in its persona, since this can be used in social causes, such as social marketing itself - which seeks to influence the behaviour of a certain target audience, with the aim of improving society's well-being in the long term (MARK; PEARSON, 2001, p.113). This reflection was reinforced when we analysed the cases of actions proposed by Pref's. In the actions we analysed, it became clear to us that Pref's takes on this role when it positions itself as the one that does good for people[74] . As the creation of a persona is part of the strategic context of Digital Marketing actions by private companies that operate on digital social networks, we deduced that Pref's brought the marketing of the private environment to the public environment, which culminated in concrete results in its actions.

The second factor we analysed as a pillar of Pref's work is the theoretical basis. It was possible to point to theoretical concepts in this research that have contributed to understanding how Pref's can achieve its objectives. The point of convergence between these concepts is that they have been used in the process of constructing the messages published and the actions proposed by Pref's. One of them, propagability, has already been discussed above. We therefore highlight two other authors (and their respective concepts) as the basis for building Pref's content.

Stuart Hall (2003) was identified by us during the research as a theorist whose Encoding and Decoding model can be used to analyse Pref's approach on digital social networks. In the publications posted, mainly on Pref's Facebook page, it was possible to observe the process of information circulation in which the message was codified by Pref's team and inserted into a repertoire that could be recognised by its followers, thus being translated (decoded, according to Hall's concept (2003)) in a way that was closer to how it was idealised, so that it could then be propagated. We understand that the use of a repertoire recognised by the user in the messages (especially pop culture) was the way Pref's used so that the people who followed the page could decode its messages in a way that was closer to the way it was encoded. This indicates that a preferential reading was suggested to those who followed the messages. The use of the repertoire made it easier, in a way, for Pref's followers to achieve this goal.

These two theories (propagability; coding and decoding) were identified by us during the research, but we were not told by Pref's team that the concepts were applied purposefully to the messages posted. We understand that the actions (whether publications or entire campaigns) are part of a digital marketing approach normally used by companies operating in the market. This is not to say that the theoretical concepts are not valid, but they have been contextualised with Pref's work because they are part of the reflections we have had

[74] We refer here to the "Enzo Day" case, analysed in Chapter 4, when in one of the posts (image 34) the expression **The social network being used for GOOD** was published, making us think that this is a kind of self promotion by Pref's, identifying itself as the good-doer of the action.

during the construction of this dissertation. However, for one of the theories discussed in this dissertation, we were informed that it was an effective theoretical basis for Pref's publications. We are referring here to Koopmans (2004).

The concepts of legitimacy, visibility and resonance are pointed out by the team itself (BORBA, 2016) as being the theoretical basis underpinning Pref's content production. These concepts are so relevant to Pref's universe that it is possible to relate them to the very existence and maintenance of the channel on the Internet. If we consider it highly legitimate for a public institution to have an active channel to deal with municipal issues, and treat a channel with an irreverent and humorous approach as highly illegitimate, we will find the point of balance; that is, the point of resonance, the very existence of a page like Pref's. There are criticisms of Pref's digital channels, such as the Facebook page Prefescura de Curitiba[75] , which opens up space for people who don't agree with Pref's approach. This disagreement can be exemplified by the mascot of the city of Curitiba. Due to Pref's success on digital social networks, the capybara became nationally known as the city's mascot. This reference was confirmed with the launch of various products with the capybara as their theme in a chain of souvenir shops in Curitiba[76] . On the other hand, the city council decreed as law (in 2010) that the city's official mascot is a bird called the Grimpeiro .[77]

We therefore agree that this dichotomy theorised by Koopmans (2004) and applied by the Pref's team in their posts and also present in the very existence of Pref's is responsible for the large reach of people that Pref's has achieved.

Finally, another factor that we pointed out as a basis for Pref's is Relationship. From the start of our research, relationships were part of our questions and hypotheses about the communication process. After all the research we've done, it's clear to us that it is indeed significant for the realisation of actions proposed through communication. If we look at the Pref's actions analysed in Chapter 4 of this dissertation, we can certainly find signs that the actions (blood and bone marrow donations and the identification of a donor with rare blood) were carried out because Pref's established a relationship with its followers, who ended up becoming replicators of the published content, as well as many of them possibly adhering to the campaigns, given that many published photos after making the donations (see ANNEX I, Enzo Day campaign, p. 12-13).

The search for this relationship is the end of the process that began with the other factors mentioned above. It was necessary to create a persona that would be recognised by its audience and referenced by this

---

[75] The page is a channel whose main objective is to point out the things that aren't going right in the city of Curitiba, as well as explicitly criticising the Pref's behaviour on digital social networks. The page has more than 20,000 followers (likes) at the time of writing. Its content can be visited at: https://www.facebook.com/prefrescuradecuritiba accessed on 22/10/2016.

[76] Article featuring the capybara as Curitiba's official mascot. Available at https://www.bemparana.com.br/noticia/395702/mascote-oficial-de-curitiba-capivara-vira-sucesso-de- sales accessed on 22/10/2016.

[77] Article citing the law referred to in the text and identifying the **Grimpeiro** bird, Curitiba's official mascot. Available at http://livre.jor.br/mascote-oficial-de-curitiba-e-o-passaro-grimpeiro-pia-capivara/ accessed on 22/10/2016.

personality; then it was necessary to ensure that this persona's posts reached as many people as possible, so the content was based on theoretical concepts (direct or indirect). All this in order to establish a relationship with its citizens through digital social networks. The result was so significant that other town halls tried to follow Pref's model, giving rise to the expression "Prefstisation", which received the following comment (figure 40) from one of Pref's pioneers, publicist Marcel Bely .[78]

The point we want to emphasise in Bely's post is the fact that messages are signified. In our understanding, this process of signification is the search for a relationship. From the moment the message is understood by the user of a digital social network, we understand that a relationship has been established.
We therefore conclude that the relationship that Pref's has built up with its followers has been used as a communication strategy so that messages can be understood and actions realised. We agree with Bruno Scartozzoni's (2015) statement:

> I understand the criticisms levelled at the Prefs website. In some ways it's a virtual extension of a public space and, therefore, there's that notion that public spaces should be impersonal, serious places that look like offices. Basically, the Prefs website is criticised because the taxpayer is paying for the time of a team that uses it to make jokes. But, on the other hand, the jokes that

they do, to this day, have proved to be efficient from the point of view of communication. Much more effective than if it were something serious, with the appearance of an office. (Online)

Follow

Sobre o fenômeno da "prefstização" dos órgãos municipais do país e algumas considerações:

- A maior preocupação da equipe de conteúdo em redes sociais da Prefeitura de Curitiba era sempre a de significar as postagens. Ou seja, a zoeira era apenas o meio, e não o fim, para chamar atenção para a mensagem que estava embutida ali.

- Um exemplo claro desse ponto importante acima foi o "casamento" entre as prefeituras de Curitiba e Rio de Janeiro. Tudo poderia terminar apenas sendo mais um mash-up entre páginas, como ainda ocorre por essas bandas. A nossa preocupação em trazer sempre uma mensagem nos fez ir a fundo até chegar na solução: doação de sangue e lista de ações sociais.

- A equipe de atendimento ao munícipe, na Prefeitura de Curitiba, é maior que qualquer outra. E isso não é atoa.

Like · Comment · Share

Figure 40 Screenshot of Marcel Bely's post commenting on Prefstisation.
Source:http://www.wegov.net.br/a-prefstizacao-dos-orgaos-publicos/ Accessed on 22/10/2016

Obviously, Pref's and any other digital social media page cannot be unanimous. However, it is undeniable that Pref's unusual and irreverent behaviour has pleased many people and contributed to public institutions (and even private ones) seeking to reinvent themselves and devise new strategies for their digital channels. Pref's can be considered an example of action on digital social networks, as it achieved a significant

[78] Marcel Bely was part of Pref's first team. He currently works on content for social networks at his own agency. Available at http://www. meioemensagem. com.br/home/ultimas- noticias/2016/06/02/idealizadores-da-prefs-de-curitiba-lancam-queen-content.html Accessed 22/10/2016.

result in the number of likes on its Facebook page (as described in the graph in chapter 2 of this dissertation). It is uncertain whether the work carried out by Pref's will continue (or how it will continue), since the mayor who was in office when the department was created was not re-elected .[79]

In fact, the work carried out by Pref's offers a legacy to those who intend to develop actions in digital social networks, especially through studies such as those carried out in this master's research. We hope that, like Pref's work, this research can contribute to future reflections on the work of digital marketing professionals in digital social networks, in both public and private environments.

BIBLIOGRAPHICAL REFERENCES

ALBUQUERQUE, Aline. The housing issue in Curitiba: the enigma of the model city. Master's thesis presented to the Faculty of Architecture and Urbanism at the University of São Paulo. 2007

ARISTOTLE. Politics. 1st edition. Translated by Torrieri Guimarães. São Paulo: Editora Martin Claret, 2002

BARCELLOS, Paulo Fernando Pinto. The financial value of customer satisfaction: reflections at a macro and microeconomic level. In: MILAN, Gabriel Sperandio;

BAUMAN, Z. Liquid love: on the fragility of human bonds. Rio de Janeiro: Jorge Zahar Editor, 2004.

BOGMANN, Itzhak Meir, Marketing de relacionamento: estratégia de fidelização e suas implicações financeiras, São Paulo: Nobel, 2002.

BORBA, Álvaro. Interview given to Luciano Giannini by email on 28/03/2016

BRANDÃO, Elizabeth Pazito. Public Communication. XXI BRAZILIAN CONGRESS OF COMMUNICATION SCIENCES. Recife, September 1998. In: ENAP - National School of Public Administration. Public Communication Course. Workbook. June and July 2005.

CASTELLS, Manuel (1999). The Information Age: Economy, Society and Culture, vol. 3. São Paulo: Paz e terra.

CESAR, A. M. R. V. C. . Case Studies or Teaching Cases? An analysis of the two methods in teaching and research in administration. REMAC Revista Eletrônica Mackenzie de Casos, São Paulo - Brazil, v. 1, n. 1, 2005.

COELHO NETTO, J. T. Semiótica, informação e comunicação. São Paulo: Perspectiva, 1996.

COBERTURA, Enzo Day:
Banda B Curitiba: http://www.bandab.com.br/jornalismo/campanha-enzo-day- incentiva-doacao-medula-ossea-curitiba/ 2016
G1 Paraná: http://g1.globo.com/pr/parana/noticia/2014/02/campanha- para-doacao-de-medula-ossea-leva-315-pessoas-ao-hemepar.html. 2016
Bem Paraná : http://www.bemparana.com.br/noticia/306246/campanha- enzo-day-registers-315-new-marrow-donors 2016
Band FM: http://bandnewsfmcuritiba.com/hemepar-realiza-amanha- enzo-day-to-register-marrow-donors

[79] At the time of finalising this dissertation, there had been no decision as to whether the department would continue due to the change in the Mayor of Curitiba.

2016

DENTON, D. Keith. Quality in services: customer service as a factor in competitive advantage. São Paulo: Makron Books, 1990.

DUARTE, J. Public communication instrument. In: DUARTE, Jorge (Org.). Comunicação pública: estado, mercado, sociedade e interesse público. São Paulo: Atlas, 2007.

EBERLE, Luciene; MILAN, Gabriel Sperandio. Identifying the dimensions of quality in services: a study applied to a higher education institution located in Caxias do Sul-RS. Caxias do Sul, RS, 2009. 147 f. Dissertation (Master's) - University of Caxias do Sul, Postgraduate Programme in Administration, 2009.

FACHIN, Odília. Fundamentals of methodology. São Paulo: Saraiva. 2001.

FRANÇA, Vera V, SIMOES, P.G. Interação - In Research Group on Image and Sociability (GRIS) : trajectory, concepts and research in communication / Organisation Vera Veiga França, Bruno Guimarães Martins, André Melo Mendes. Belo Horizonte : Faculty of Philosophy and Human Sciences - PPGCom - UFMG, 2015.

GARCIA, Sheila F. A. Temas de Administração Pública, v. 2, n.3. UNESP - Universidade Estadual Paulista. Faculty of Sciences and Letters - Department of Public Administration. Araraquara - SP - Brazil. 2008

GABRIEL, Martha. Marketing in the digital age: concepts, platforms and strategies. São Paulo: Novatec, 2010.

GALINDO Daniel dos S. Comunicação Mercadológica uma revisão conceptual in Comunicação Institucional e Mercadológica - Expansões conceptituais e Imbricações temáticas, organised by Daniel S. Galindo, São Bernardo do Campo: Editora metodista, 2012.

GALINDO, Daniel. O sujeito Social em sua persona de consumidor em re(ação) in Gonçalvez, Elizabeth Moraes [org] Práticas comunicacionais: sujeitos em re(ação). São Bernardo do Campo: Methodist University of São Paulo, 2013.

GOFFMAN, Erving. The representation of the self in everyday life. Petrópolis: Vozes, 2002

GOMES, W. Internet and political participation. In: GOMES, W.; MAIA, R.C.M. Comunicação e Democracia: Problemas e perspectivas. São Paulo: Paulus, 2008, p. 293324.

GONÇALVES, Elizabeth Moraes. Organisations and the new public-private visibility. In. BUENO, Wilson da Costa. (org.) Communication Strategies in Social Media. São Paulo
Paulo: Manole, 2015.

GRANOVETTER, M. The Strength of Weak Ties. The American Journal of Sociology, vol. 78, n. 6, p. 1360-1380, May 1973.

GRONROOS, Christian. Marketing: management and services: the competition for services at the moment of truth. 5. ed. Rio de Janeiro: Campus, 1999.

_____ . Marketing: management and services. 2. ed. Rio de Janeiro: Elsevier, 2004.

GUEDES, Éllida Neiva (2010). Contemporary public space: plurality of voices and interests. Available at: http://www.bocc.ubi.pt/pag/guedes-ellida-espaco-publico- contemporaneo.pdf

HABERMAS, Jurgen. Structural change in the public sphere. Rio de Janeiro: Tempo Brasileiro, 1984.

HALL, Stuart. Encoding/Decoding. In: HALL, Stuart, Da diáspora: Identidades e medições culturais. Belo Horizonte, UFMG, 2003.

HOFFMAN, K. Douglas; BATESON, John E. G. Principles of services marketing: concepts, strategies and cases. São Paulo: Thomson, 2003.

IAN, Gordon. Relationship marketing: strategies, techniques and technologies to win customers and keep them forever. 1. ed. São Paulo: Futura, 1999.

JENKINS, Henry. Convergence culture. São Paulo: Aleph, 2006.

_______ GREEN, Joshua; FORD, Sam. Culture of Connection. São Paulo: Editora ALEPH, 2014

KANT, I. Critique of the Faculty of Judgement, transl. Valério Rohden and Antônio Marques, Rio de Janeiro: Forense Universitária, 2008

KOOPAMNS, Ruud. Movements and media: Selection processes and evolutionary dynamics in the public sphere In: Theory and Society 33: 367-391, 2004.

KOTLER, Philip. Marketing management: analysis, planning, implementation and control. 5. ed. São Paulo: Atlas, 1998.

_____ . Marketing management: the new millennium edition. São Paulo: Prentice Hall, 2000.

_____ ; KELLER, Kevin Lane. Marketing management. 12. ed. São Paulo: Pearson Prentice Hall, 2006

LÉVY, P. Collective intelligence: towards an anthropology of cyberspace. 3.ed. São Paulo: Loyola, 2000

LIMA, João S. PÓLIS E POLITEÍA IN ARISTÓTELES A study on the ethics of citizenship in Politics. Thesis presented to the Institute of Philosophy and Human Sciences of the State University of Campinas, for the degree of Doctor of Philosophy. Campinas, 2010

MCCOMBS, M.; SHAW, D. The agenda-setting function of mass media. Public Opinion Quaterly, v. 36, n. 2, p. 176-182, summer 1972.

MARK, Margaret. PEARSON, Carol. The Hero and the Outlaw. São Paulo: Cultrix, 2001.

MARTINO, Luis Mauro Sá. Digital Media Theory, Languages, Environments and Networks. Petrópolis: Vozes, 2014

MARX, Karl. Introduction [to the Critique of Political Economy]. In: _______ . For the Critique of political economy. Translation by Edgar Malagodi et al. São Paulo: Abril Cultural, 1982.

McKENNA, Regis. Relationship marketing. Rio de Janeiro: Campus, 1993

MCQUAIL, Denis. Theory of Mass Communication. Porto Alegre: Penso, 2013

MEZZOMO, Augusto Antonio. Hospital humanisation: anthropological and technological foundations. São Paulo: Loyola, 2010.

MILLER, Daniel & SLATER, Don. "Ethnography on and offline: internet cafés in Trinidad". Horizons

Anthropological, v. 1, n. 21, year 10, p. 41-65. 2004

NETO, Marcem ques. The 4 Rs of Public Relations. Available at: https://versatilrp.com.br/2012/06/29/os-4-rs-das-relacoes-publicas-por-marcem ques- neto/ Accessed on 05/07/2016

NOBRE, Jorge Alberto. Your excellence the customer: quality in service. 7. ed. Porto Alegre: Passaporte para o sucesso, 2003.

WHAT IS EdgeRank? Available at: http://www.academiadomarketing.com.br/o- que-e-edgerank/ Accessed on 12/04/2016

PEPPERS, D.; Rogers, M. One-to-one marketing: Individualised marketing in the age of the customer. Editora Campus, 1994.

__________. One-to-One Web Marketing Overview. In: One-to-One Web Marketing: Build a Relationship Marketing Strategy One by Cliff Allen,Deborah Kania,Beth Yaeckel Org. New York, Weley, 2001

__________. Managing Custumer Relationships. New York, Weley, 2004

WHY IS IT much better to create a Facebook Page for your business? Available at: https://www.facebook.com/business/news/BR-Por-que-e-muito-melhor-criar-uma- Facebook-Page-for-your-business Accessed on 22/10/2016

PORTO, Mauro P. Research on reception and media effects: proposing an integrated approach. XXVI Brazilian Congress of Communication Sciences. INTERCOM, Belo Horizonte, MG. Proceedings... 2-6, September 2003.

PRAZERES, Paulo Mundin. Dictionary of quality terms. São Paulo: Atlas, 1996

PRIMO, Alex. Computer-mediated interaction: communication, cyberculture, cognition. Porto Alegre: Sulina, 2007.

____ . The relational aspect of interactions in Web 2.0. E-Compós, v. 9, pp. 1-21, Brasília, 2007.

WHEN IS IT worth boosting posts on Facebook? Available at: http://nrcm.net/revistaexame . Accessed on 08/08/2016).

RECUERO, Raquel. Considerations on the Diffusion of Information in Social Networks on the Internet. Paper presented at the Intercom South Congress. Passo Fundo, 2007. Available at: http://nrcm.net/Considerações on the Dissemination of Information on Social Networks on the Internet

_________Raquel da Cunha. Social networks on the Internet. Porto Alegre: Sulina, 2009

ROBERTS, Kevin. Lovemarks: The future beyond brands, M. Books, 2004.

ROCHA, E. C.; GOMES, S. H. A. Gestão da qualidade em unidades de informação. Ciência da Informação, Brasília, DF, v. 22, n. 2, p. 142-52, 1993.

SANTAELLA, Lucia. What is Semiotics: First Steps Collection. São Paulo: Ed. Brasiliense, 2003.

SAMPAIO, Rafael C. Digital Democracy in Brazil: a prospection of relevant initiatives. **In:** Revista Eletrônica de Ciência Política, vol. 4, n. 1-2, 2013.

SCARTOZZONI, Bruno. Interview with the portal http://www.wegov.net.br/a-prefstizacao- dos-orgaos-publicos/. 2015

SHIOZAWA, Ruy Sergio Cacese. Quality in customer service and information technology. São Paulo: Atlas, 2003.

SILVA, Patricia dos Santos Caldas. Challenges of human development in the management of public organisations. In: KUNSCH, Margarida (org). Communication as a factor in humanising organisations. São Caetano do Sul, SP: Difusão, 2010. (Series Pensamento e Prática; v.3.)

TOFFLER, Alvin. The third wave. Translated by João Távora. 32nd ed. Rio de Janeiro: Record, 2014.

TURCHI, Sandra (2013). Brand Persona: An Important Part of Social Media Strategy. Available at: http://ecommercenews.com.br/artigos/cases/persona-da-marca- important-part-of-social-media-strategy accessed on 21/04/2016.

WEBSTER, Jr., F. The changing role of marketing in the corporation. Journal of Marketing, v. 56. n. 3, p. 1-17, 1992.

WOLTON, Dominique. Internet, so what? A critical theory of the new media. Porto Alegre: Sulina, 2003.

___ (2005), In: MONTARDO, S. P., Praise of radical humanism. Interview with Dominique Wolton, Revista FAMECOS, Porto Alegre no 27, August 2005, available at: http://revistaseletronicas.pucrs.br/ojs/index.php/revistafamecos/article/view/3316/2575 Accessed on 20/04/2016

YIN, Robert K. Case study - planning and methods (2Ed.). Porto Alegre: Bookman. 2001.

YIN, Robert K. Applications of case study research. Thousand Oaks, California: Sage Publications. 1993.

Printed by Books on Demand GmbH, Norderstedt / Germany